the slow guide

HELEN HAWKES & LETA KEENS

PHOTOGRAPHY BY OLIVER STREWE

AFFirM press

Published by Affirm Press in 2007
Corner of Wellington and Jacksons Roads, Mulgrave, Vic 3170

National Library of Australia
Cataloguing-in-Publication Entry

Hawkes, Helen.
The slow guide to Sydney.

Includes index.
ISBN 9780980374612 (pbk).

1. Sydney (NSW) - Guidebooks. I. Keens, Leta. II. Strewe, Oliver. III. Egger, Simone. IV. Title. (Series: Slow guides; 2).

919.44104

Designed by Sense Advertising & Design
Printed by McPherson's Printing

Disclaimer

All reasonable steps were taken – allowing for bad days, personal dramas, distractions and frequent lie-downs – to ensure that all the information in this book is accurate and up to date. Apologies if we've missed anything.

People to thank

Helen Hawkes wishes to thank Tony Dymond for the bird advice, Martyn Robinson from the Australian Museum, PR Stewart White, author Nikki Goldstein, the whole Cipri family but especially the ultra charming Carmelo, Dawson Oughton at the Royal Botanic Gardens and Martin Hughes for the chance to be involved in the book. Leta Keens wishes to add Louise Pfanner, Michael Fitzgerald and Paul Paech. Oliver Strewe thanks all the people who let him photograph their lives, his extended Bondi family and particularly Bridget for her extraordinary skills preparing these photos for press.

From the Publisher

Affirm Press is committed to publishing books that have a positive impact on the community; that influence by delight rather than being earnest or 'right on'. The Slow Guides is our first foray, a series that may not get past its first two titles, *Melbourne* and *Sydney*, or which might become a publishing phenomenon that extends to the fastest places on earth. We'll see.

The original idea for the Slow Guides came from a friend Sally Steward who died a few years ago. It was developed by Martin Hughes, an occasional stresshead who is also kind of the publisher, along with his boss, friend and mentor Graeme Wise. Anything *but* a slow hand clap to all the contributors of this book, without whose patience and energy it would never have come together.

About this Book

The Slow Guide to Sydney was written by Helen Hawkes and Leta Keens, and photographed by Oliver Strewe.

Helen is one of Australia's foremost lifestyle journalists, and has written for most major magazines and newspapers in the country. She is a former deputy editor of *Cosmopolitan* and a section editor at the *Sun Herald*. She has also worked in London and, more disreputably, as a nightclub hostess. She is a qualified counsellor and her book, *Sex, Optimism and Surviving the 21st Century*, was published in Australia and the US.

Leta is a freelance journalist who has contributed to many publications here and internationally on subjects including travel, art, architecture, music and design. She has also contributed to two books – *New York Journal* with English journalist Liz Corcoran, and *Exposure* with photographer Jason Loucas to raise funds for the Ovarian Cancer Research Foundation.

Wendy Howitt wrote the Small chapter, a slow guide specifically for kids, and Mickey Hawkes, Glenda Morgan and Andrew Hobbs contributed essays on their respective passions.

Oliver is one of the coolest, calmest cats we know. He has been working as a photographer since the early 1970s, around the time he moved to Bondi. He works extensively throughout Australia and overseas, which is why he can do 'love' jobs like this. He recently published a book of stunning photographs on the *Beaches, Bays & Coves of Sydney*.

Simone Egger edited, while long-time Mr Reliable Pete Cruttenden proofed and Adrienne Costanzo parachuted in at the last minute to do the index. Sense Design's Guillaume Roux, Oleg Fedotov and Stephen Walker looked after the design and layout, while Jakub Jablonski provided many of the illustrations.

Local

Natural

Traditional

SENSORY

Characteristic

Contents

A Slow Start

In the eighties, greed was good. In the noughties, speed is often the altar at which we are urged to worship. Popular media is obsessed with the idea of 'now, now, now' and 'next, next, next' and, caught up in this sentiment, it seems our lives can't help but be tuned to the pursuit of 'fast'.

At work, we labour under the demands of time or, rather, *no* time: we have to get the report into the boss by Friday, be up the freeway by 6pm or at lunch by 1pm sharp. At home, we often find little time to 'relax' beyond television or computer games, and sate our hunger with 'convenience' foods. Increasingly, our leisure time is eaten up with work or chores that allows little time to indulge in sensory and simple pleasures?

Yet, encouragingly, there is growing conviction that life should be more than a rush from A to B. That we should savour the sounds and sights of the environment and culture in which we find ourselves. That our food should be organic and lovingly prepared; that our exercise should involve nature and long, slow strolls; that our entertainment and commerce should embrace genuine interaction with other members of our community; and that, rather than our lives being ruled by the clocks on our gadgets, the seasons should at least play a role in guiding the rhythm of our lives.

The word 'slow' is used 56

we didn't get around to. Little wonder that many of us can feel like we're on a treadmill that keeps going faster and faster.

Whether it's urbanisation, consumerism, technology or globalisation, the truth is everything has become a race to the finish line – with a price. In Sydney, the toll of busyness is everywhere.

There is no doubt that stress, depression, road accidents and chronic misery are in part related to our go-faster, achieve-more philosophy. How many of us can really maintain the hectic pace that is demanded of those who want to 'succeed'? And, indeed, what does success mean in a culture or environment

I guess that's where the idea for this book came in. The *Slow Guide* is the book that we always wished we had, a city guide in praise of wonderful, rich, soul-tingling slowness. A guide that reveals the best places in the city to reconnect with your passion for food, handmade fashion or gifts, architecturally stunning buildings or parks that are brimming with flora and fauna.

It's not a tourist guide or indeed a definitive guide to 'the biggest, the boldest, the best'. This book is about the farmers' market or the heritage building you may never have visited; the vintage fashion shop that holds a hundred bargains you'll fall in love with; the secret cove where you can picnic with a lover or just play boy scout – or girl guide.

Simply put, it's about going slowly enough to discover the joys of the city and going places where speed doesn't rule.

What exactly is slow, you ask? Well, most simply, it's the opposite to fast. It's about arousing the senses, connecting with the community, taking comfort in the natural world and ultimately living happier and healthier lives.

In an age where sea-changing and tree-changing sometimes feel like the only ways off the merry-go-round, the *Slow Guide* is meant as a manual for managing to get more

As we discovered while writing this book, we live in a city that absolutely vibrates with nature, culture, humanity and joy. If you haven't played hooky for a day recently, or ever taken a holiday in your own city, then may we suggest that the time is ripe and the tool is in your hands.

Some suggestions: go to your favourite beach – check out little known destinations such as Turimetta or Store Beach – and search for flotsam or shells. Find a cafe that nourishes more than with food, and settle in for a spell. Take time to buy something handmade and wonderful, or something vintage and collectable, and talk to the person in

times throughout this book

out of the life you have now. It's for people attracted to the idea of downshifting but who actually like where they work and live – who love the buzz and richness of the city, but want to take it at their own pace.

Don't get us wrong. We're not Luddites and we're certainly not saying that new is bad or that trendy should be spurned. We're about taking what is new (everything from food to fashion) and what is old (architecture, historic sites and timeless coves) and combining it with slow values to improve our quality of life. The *Slow Guide* is about turning down the speed meter enough to appreciate all the good things we have in Sydney.

the shop about where it comes from or how it was made.

You'll find everything you need to ignite or reignite your love affair with Sydney. And who knows? The *Slow Guide* may become not just a passport to, but a symbol for, a new and more pleasurable way of living in Sydney.

We hope this book hits the mark, arouses your senses, fires your enthusiasm and nurtures your soul, even just a little. Within its pages are secrets. Indeed, this book holds the key to a new city experience, one that more and more of us believe we should have. Happy living in the city.

HELEN HAWKES

Character

WHAT SHAPES SYDNEY AND ITS PEOPLE

TIME
Against the Clock

- • -

" HOW WE SPEND OUR DAYS
IS HOW WE SPEND OUR LIVES. "

Pulitzer Prize–winning author Annie Dillard

time

nature

Although we get materially wealthier and technologically more advanced, one thing that seems in ever-diminishing supply is time. Perhaps the pace of modern life makes it more difficult to slow down. We're living in a world where instant gratification is not fast enough; in a world of speed dating, email and microwave meals. Days aren't getting shorter but we're increasingly hard-pressed to find moments for ourselves. Technology was sold to us with the idea it would give us more leisure but, ironically, hooked up to computers, mobile phones and BlackBerrys, we find there isn't enough time.

"Time hasn't changed – our interpretation of it has," says Doug Minty, a clockmaker and repairer, lifelong collector of timepieces and a former Sydney president of the National Association of Watch and Clock Collectors. "We have clocks on our computer, clocks on our mobile phones and clocks on our microwaves. But rather than helping us manage time, we let these devices control us," he says. "We are always rushing to beat time. We have flexi time that is supposed to let busy people go on holiday, or overtime when people cram even more work into their week."

"The time-and-motion people have taken over," says Richard Waterhouse, Bicentennial Professor of Australian History at the University of Sydney. "We all run around because of these ultramodern ideas about what makes people efficient, based on economics and psychology."

We no longer work to live, we work to maintain our 'lifestyle', he says. "People's expectations are much higher than they were 20 years ago. They want the big home, the air-conditioning, the new car, the latest audio-visual equipment, the mobile phone…and they are willing to sacrifice all kinds of things for them, including time."

By contrast, the Sydney of old didn't encourage this kind of high-earning, high-accumulation mentality, which has us always trying to beat the clock. "From 1788 when Sydney was settled until the early 1850s, clock time didn't mean very much to people. Work was done according to the task," says Waterhouse. Then, in the 1850s, the Eight Hour Movement sprung up. "'Eight hours' work, eight hours' rest and eight hours for what you will' was the slogan," he says.

Take a leap forward to the 1970s, when we abolished Saturday midday closing and, then, onwards to the deregulation of working hours, and it's not too difficult to see where time has gone.

Yet what exactly is time? You may believe it is the force that drives the mad rush to get everything done on a competitive level. But the reality is infinitely more beautiful and, dare we say it, timeless, says Minty: "It is a concept based on Nature and lunar cycles…as the rains come, the crops sprout green and birds migrate for the winter, so time moves in our own lives."

Is time a force we're constantly pushing against, to be more productive, competitive or happy? Or is it the wondrous cycle of the natural world? Does time sound like tick-tock and beep-beep, or the dawn chorus of birds singing and nocturnal creatures scurrying? Does it have a little-hand and a big-hand, or does it look like the changing light as the sun comes up, moves across the sky, and goes back down again?

For a romantic view of time, and not one that would be favoured by time-and-motion experts, walk to the herb gardens in the Royal Botanic Gardens and take a look at the 2.4m silicon bronze armillary sphere sundial that features herbs modelled in relief. Waste a little time by stopping to smell the basil and bay leaf and rosemary too.

Sadly, sundials never really took off in the 'real' world. Their measurement of time is, perhaps, simply too fluid. Yet, before the introduction of standard time, every municipality in the civilised world set its official clock to the position of the sun. Standard time, where all clocks in a large region were set to the same time, was established in the late 1800s. Today, 300 atomic clocks in more than 50 laboratories worldwide, are used to set Universal Time, says Minty. They are accurate to one second in 3000 years, making it impossible, it would seem, for time to ever slip away from us, or for us to escape the demands of time. "We can't control time but time controls us," says Minty. "Even on holiday we don't switch off."

The good news is that "there is a movement against the new fast pace by which we live our lives," says Waterhouse. "Of course it is the Slow Movement and it is also the grey nomads in their travelling vans and the seachangers and treechangers and everyone else who says 'I can't keep this up anymore' or, more definitively, 'I don't want to'."

Because for all the devices that would attempt to tell us exactly what moment of the millennium we stand in now, we have another natural, in-built mechanism that can more accurately guide the passage of our lives. It is called our heart and it is the human timepiece that measures how well we live. If it is full, we know that we have been using time wisely. If it is empty, we should forget about watches and mobile phones and speed dating and microwave meals and instead focus on spending time with those we care about, including ourselves, in places that we care about.

We should take the time, have time off, lose track of time and look at all the other ways we can thumb our noses at those who would point at their watches and admonish our need to go slow.

**BE HAPPY WHILE YOU ARE LIVING
FOR YOU'RE A LONG TIME DEAD.**

Scottish proverb

Time in Eternity

If you had to choose a view on which to gaze for eternity, why not the oceanic panorama that can be viewed from a plot at Waverley Cemetery. Looking out to sea, surrounded by the final resting place of some of the city's most famous residents, it is easy to feel that time is both endless and yet swift in passing. There is a stillness here, a peacefulness apart from the buzz of city life in surrounding suburbs, even though the busy suburb of Bondi is only minutes away.

In 39 acres rest some 50,000 souls. Many still linger among us in name, like JF Archibald (1856–1919) after whom the famous portrait prize is named or poet Dorothea Mackellar (1885–1967) who wrote the immortal words: "I love a sunburnt country, a land of sweeping plains…" Others, like colourful Sydney racing identity George Freeman (1935–90), have enjoyed more than their 15 minutes of fame. Some have been robbed of time – early settlers who arrived hoping for a paradise but died of exotic disease or in childbirth; soldiers who fought in the Civil War.

The cemetery is also host to families who come to spend moments with loved ones and acknowledge time's passing. Marking dates on our non-natural calendars of time: the 4th of July brings an influx of Americans who remember soldiers from the K10 regiment, and the anniversary of the Fenian Rising of 1867 is commemorated at the Irish Martyr's Memorial inscribed "who fears speak of ninety eight, who blushes at the name".

Other less-celebrated graves are no less a reminder that human flesh may be subject to a biological ticking but that some things outlast time. Among the headstones of marble and stone, the vaults that contain generations of Italians and the scrub that grows between the graves, an inscription reads: "Love hands about thy name like music round a shell. No heart can take of them or time farewell."

Time and Place

Dawn

Flying into Sydney, when the plane has the best flight path – straight up between the Heads – is the best way to start a Sydney day we say. Everything's in black and white, and the headlands are marked out in silhouette like a David Moore photo, but the harbour shimmers like silver, and coming home is a treat.

Near Warwick Farm Racecourse when the horses get their early-morning exercise is another bright start. They've spent the night in the equivalent of a very smart equine motel (on a side street just a gentle trot away from the racecourse), and now is the time for some work. Try it one morning in winter, when there's dew on the grass and condensation drifting from the horses' nostrils. And marvel at the stamina of the strappers and trainers who get up this early every day.

Morning

Head to Auburn, the heart of Sydney's Turkish community, and start your day with a coffee and *simit* (delicious sweet-salty pastry covered in sesame seeds) at Mado on Auburn Rd, then go on a shopping spree around the delis and

Mindfulness

Life in the city can seem like an endless treadmill of rushing from A to B. The pace seems to us to be frenetic and, for some, too much to keep up with. "As a result many people try to change the outside world to suit how they feel," says Sydneysider Stuart Mackay, who has been teaching meditation for 25 years through his company Peace At Work. "But the secret is to change the inside. Where there is focus there is peace."

He suggests Sydneysiders who want to find a slower pace concentrate first on slowing the rush of thoughts through their brain. "A quiet mind is the most powerful key you can possess," says Mackay.

In daily life, make a conscious effort to slow your pace – walk more slowly, take the slow train, ride a bike – and concentrate on one thing at a time. Bring mindfulness to everything you do and you will soon find that you not only appreciate experiences more but you also have a lot less stress.

The next step is to add a meditation practice to your day. You don't have to be a guru. You just need to devote 10 minutes to it, in the morning or at night. To make a start, go to www.peaceatwork.com, click on 'sample' and try the free meditation exercise that you can use in your everyday life. Be quiet. Be slow. Be alive.

bakeries in the area. Some of the best things include olive paste, figs and dates, Turkish fairy floss, sour cherry juice and Turkish jams. Pick up a traditional lucky talisman, a blue glass eye, and visit the Gallipoli Mosque if it happens to be open.

Victoria Barracks in Paddington is edifying on a Thursday or Sunday morning (the only two days they're open to the public). The spectacular buildings, centred on a huge parade ground, were made of locally quarried sandstone in the 1840s and occupied by British troops until 1870. Troops heading to Sudan were trained here in 1885 and the buildings have housed various army units ever since. And if you're that way inclined, you may just stumble into the ghost of Private Crowley of the 11th North Devonshire Regiment, who's believed to hang around the museum area.

Midday

Visit St James Church at the top of King St to enjoy the fine combination of colonial architecture and enchanting music. Built in 1824, it is the oldest church in the city. Strangely enough, it was designed as a courthouse but, before construction started, the nifty addition of a spire radically changed its function. Lunchtime concerts happen most Wednesdays, with entry by donation.

Savour somewhere shaded – the Fernery at the Royal Botanic Gardens is a pretty good bet (it's nice and airy as well), but otherwise relax on a bench in Hyde Park, along the gorgeous avenue of fig trees. Some have succumbed to a soil disease and have had to be chopped down, and quite a few more are in danger, so make the most of them while you can.

Afternoon

Catch a film at the Art Gallery of New South Wales. They usually start in the early afternoon a couple of times a week and tie in loosely with major exhibitions. For instance, during an exhibition of German artist Anselm Kiefer's work, there was a mini-festival of German films, and lots of Middle Eastern movies during the Arts of Islam. If you're in the mood for extra intellectual stimulation, book up for one of the Art Gallery's courses, which could be anything from an introduction to philosophy to a look at the arts of Asia.

At the Gunners' Barracks, which is set in bushland at Georges Head overlooking Chowder Bay in Mosman, you can book yourself in for a completely indulgent afternoon tea. The sandstone buildings that make up the old barracks were designed by colonial architect James Barnet in 1873, and were used by the military for many different purposes 130 years before their latest transformation. What the top brass would say of the move from bully beef to scones and champagne, though, is anyone's guess.

Evening

In the city, watch thousands of birds congregate around the lights at the top of the bridge and the AMP Building for their almost obscene feeding frenzy. Bugs are attracted to light, and birds like nothing better than an insect dinner – these spots are the McDonald's of the avian world. Or visit a local park for a picnic dinner. You don't have to save eating alfresco for weekends and holidays – just break the routine every now and then and you'll be surprised how relaxed it makes you feel.

Dusk

Victoria St in Potts Point, above the naval car park, is the place to watch the nightly migration of the flying foxes. You'll hear the gentle beat of thousands of pairs of wings, and hear the chatter and squawks as they form a benevolent dark cloud in the sky above you.

Or hop aboard the Manly ferry. You'll probably get caught up with commuters, but that's OK: they're a happier lot than those who have to use trains and buses to make their way to and from work. And why wouldn't they be, when they can smell sea spray, watch the lights gradually come on in harbourside suburbs as the sun goes down and follow the gulls trailing in the ferry's wake, getting a very real sense of the weather, feeling the heave of the swell, and every now and then seeing a migrating humpback whale making a guest appearance on their commuter route?

After Dark

Wander down to Old South Head Rd to watch the beacon flashing every 10 seconds and carrying 25 nautical miles out to sea, at Australia's oldest lighthouse. Well, it's almost the oldest – the current and very handsome Macquarie Lighthouse was built in the 1880s, very similar to convict Francis Greenway's original design, which had been built in 1818 of poor quality sandstone quarried from the site. It was so bad, in fact, that Greenway warned Governor Macquarie, who had commissioned it, that it wouldn't last. He was right – five years later it was falling to bits and had to be strapped up. It didn't matter – Governor Macquarie was so pleased with Greenway's work that he gave him a pardon on the strength of it. ∎

A Free Day

Reclaim time. Spend a day doing nothing except lying in a hammock or sitting in a comfortable chair, listening to the sounds of nature or your favourite CDs. Turn off your mobile phone and your computer. Remove your watch. Eat cheese and fruit, and drink wine or champagne, savouring their sweet, pungent or spicy tastes as you roll them over your tongue. Take a nap. Read that book. Eat when you are hungry or doze again when sleepy. Play with your children. Play with your dog. Do whatever you feel like, with no time-piece to be your jailer. Feel that time is your own.

NATURE
Knowing our Place

- • -

" EARTH IS CRAMMED WITH HEAVEN. "

Elizabeth Barrett Browning

Sydney feels magnificently touched by the gods, where natural beauty intertwines with a unique urban environment that mixes the best of development, culture and cuisine. Its charisma comes from a shoreline that stretches to 240km and is pocked by innumerable bays and coves, a splendrous vision that has entranced everyone from the Aborigines who camped near the water to the Sydneysiders who wish they could live there today. You know your soul belongs to this place when you dream of the ocean's embrace and the vista that greets you at every twist and turn.

And that's why we celebrate Sydney's natural assets – its harbour of many accolades, its birds and mammals, its marine life – and strive to protect them from poor management and climate change. Green is the new black. A shower timer is the hottest bathroom accessory; buying drought-proof plants is hip; and, if you can afford it, a hybrid car is now a bigger status symbol than a Mercedes. Even the government is shifting and a new agency, the Department of Environment and Climate Change, was formed in 2007 to meet future challenges head on.

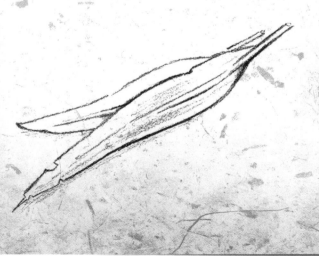

The Nature of Things

By becoming more mindful of Sydney, and appreciating it anew, we'll help to ensure a future of watching native birds flit, reclining under the shade of trees and feeling the clean, salty water of our famous harbour on our skins.

Under the Weather

The weather and our attitude to it gives Sydney a perpetual holiday feeling, which is, in reality, quite false when you consider the long hours many of its get-ahead residents now work. But the idea that, at any moment, a businessman might loosen his tie, kick off his shoes and do a little sunbathing in a nearby park plays in our imagination.

Sydney is all about summer, and a mean maximum of 21.6°C allows us to enjoy the city's most seductive pursuits like sailing, swimming and basking. It seems perpetually balmy and even on 'wintry' days we're warmed by gentle rays.

While Melburnians dash to darkened cafes for warming espressos, we love smoothies and icy-poles and ripe tropical fruits like mangoes from which we can suck the juice as the temperature soars – sometimes beyond 40°C and hotter out west without the cooling ocean breezes.

We do have rain, albeit less in the dams than we'd like. Sydney gets about 1200mm annually and about 100 days with showers. Although we increasingly welcome these occasions as drought-breakers, deep down we prefer to think of them as part of a 'tropical' climate into which a little rain must fall.

We're ill-suited to driving when it's wet – you can bet a buck you'll get held up in a bingle on the freeway when it really sleets down – and, damn it, we can't get a taxi either. It seems no one in Sydney really likes to get water on them unless it's in the ocean and, while we possess an umbrella, we never carry it. This is Sydney, not Melbourne. If there is going to be inclement weather, frankly we'd rather not know.

If anything, the constantly balmy weather has made us a little shallow. Clothes are logically skimpier so we keep our bodies in good condition. We work out at gyms or jog through parks rather than hide ourselves away in theatres or concert halls.

We show off our warm weather toys – yachts, surfboards, mountain bikes and sports cars – rather than our annual subscription to the opera or membership of the state library. Okay, we do go to the theatre or the opera – we're not plebeians, you know. But we know that life in a balmy climate is all about balance (or should that be balancing?) on a surfboard or a yacht.

Slowly, very slowly, we have learned from living under a hole in the ozone layer, and watching those scary ads on television about skin cancer, that too much sun can be a bad thing. But turn up to any Sydney beach at the peak of summer and you'll see locals and tourists alike basting themselves. Yes, sunburn is dangerous but this is 'controlled bronzing'.

Best Places to...

Go after a downpour:

- Bridge climb – from atop the famous Sydney Harbour Bridge, the brooding city is even more dramatic than in bright sunny weather.
- Taronga Zoo to watch the animals enjoy their newly soaked surroundings.
- Busby's Pond at Centennial Park, where the water birds will be having a very nice time.
- Kingfisher Pool at Heathcote National Park, when the rain creates a waterfall. But even if the cascades aren't flowing, this area of carved sandstone is one of the most stunning swimming holes around.

Wait for a cool change:

- The dark relief of a cinema: old favourite the Randwick Ritz, the beautifully restored Cremorne Orpheum, the oh-so-hip Dendy at Circular Quay and the trendy Verona or Academy Twin at Paddington.
- With your skates on at the Canterbury Olympic Ice Rink. There used to be skating rinks all over Sydney, but they're now an endangered species. Make the most of them.
- The Art Gallery of NSW – the Asian Wing is a particularly tranquil and calming part of the gallery.
- Aboard the Manly ferry – it's the easiest way to catch the sea breeze. Take your bathers with you, and head to Shelly Beach, that lovely little cove past the southern end of Manly.

Watch spectacular electrical storms:

- The Icebergs Club House at Bondi Beach (or the Icebergs Dining Room and Bar if you're feeling extravagant and in the mood to be part of a scene).
- The Gap – stormy weather just adds to the general spookiness of the place.
- The northern foyer of the Opera House. If you're lucky, you can time it for interval of an uplifting concert and really have all your senses bombarded.
- Shark or Clark Island – be prepared to get absolutely soaked to the skin, but it's worth it to watch the weather come in across the harbour, and to see how the various types of boats deal with it.
- Drink in hand at the Blu Horizon bar on the 36th floor of the Shangri-La Hotel in the Rocks.

Nature's rhythm runs through night and day. Morning has an inimitable translucent glow that declares another day of sensuality, energy and beauty. If you stop to notice. There's the sight of playful finches and sparrows taking a dry mud bath in a fig-lined park, seasonal native plants and flowers emitting pungent scents in full bloom, the slick of coconut oil and surf wax on lithe, suntanned bodies around the beaches and the bays, and the sharp, salty taste of the ocean. Most days end with a fiery amber sunset, forcing reflection and offering a reminder to take more notice tomorrow.

Mankind Versus the Environment

The ocean, the beach, the flora and fauna...these are the things that nourish us and shape our lifestyle. Of course, like all who inhabit an Eden, we too have lovers' tiffs. There's the overfishing, the fuel spewed into the waterways, the sewage that was once piped way too close to Bondi Beach and the mutilation of old trees.

In mankind-against-nature, cases of rich landowners who live ocean-side poisoning trees to enhance their view regularly hit the headlines. The irony is that trees, from Sydney to London to Sacramento, enhance property values by about 20%, says local estate agent Peter Malouf. It's no accident that Queen St, Woollahra, is one of the leafiest and most expensive streets in Sydney – thanks to the London plane.

Most recently there was much chest thumping about high levels of dioxins found in the fish that come from our harbour. Fisherfolk and their families, who regularly feed on the oceanic spoils, were found to be the most at risk. Other recent environmental scandals have included the building of an unsympathetic, multi-storied block at the Circular Quay that became known as 'the Toaster'.

Many animals are endangered or vulnerable because of intensifying development. According to Tony Dymond from the Cumberland Bird Observers' Club, there are areas where the only birds you are likely to now see are introduced Common mynahs (also known as Indian mynahs), Common starlings, Spotted turtle-doves and Rock doves. Yet some birds have adapted, like the Australian white ibis (see Birds of Sydney, page 39).

It's not all mankind *against* the environment, however. Sometimes nature bites back. Sulphur-crested cockatoos are both loved and reviled, first for their cheeky personality and plumage, second for their ability to virtually destroy an entire fruit tree in a single afternoon.

The Bluebottle, or Portuguese Man of War, is a common, if unwelcome, summer visitor to Sydney beaches that can deliver a painful sting to unwary swimmers.

Probably the most notorious of all spiders, Sydney funnel-webs, have also wreaked revenge on unwary city residents. Shiny, dark-brown to black spiders with finger-like spinnerets, they have a habit of wandering into backyards and falling into swimming pools, especially in summer and autumn while looking for a mate. If threatened, their impressive fangs can deliver one of the most toxic venoms.

While the funnel-web is probably responsible for the 13 recorded spider-bite deaths and many medically serious bites, no deaths have been recorded since the introduction of an antivenene in 1981.

As a land colonised from the sea, it's fitting that Sydney's continuing development is around the water. Governor Phillip used the freshwater Tank Stream that now runs beneath the Circular Quay (see page 154) to divide the convicts on the west from the officers on the east. Even now the east is where you'll find more of the landed gentry, while everyone else is trying to get as close to the coast as possible, or at least somewhere with 'water glimpses'.

The arrival of the land-hungry and entrepreneurial Europeans was devastating to the Aboriginal people living around the harbour and nearby areas: the Eora-, Guringai- and Daruk-speaking people. Land was cleared for camps, and forests cut down to provide fuel and building materials.

But you can still get an idea of what Sydney must have looked like before the settlers in the 393 hectares of headlands, beaches and islands that make up the Sydney Harbour National Park. You can see coastal heath and woodland that includes such rare plant species as *Eucalyptus camfieldii* (a stringybark) and the wet heath groundcover *Rulingia hermanniifolia*. At Nielsen Park, the Hermitage Foreshore and South Head, remnants of the original vegetation include Port Jackson figs, tick bush and tea tree.

For the story of the Cadigal people, the traditional Aboriginal owners of the Sydney city area, visit the Cadi Jam Ora: First Encounters garden at the Royal Botanic Gardens. It features plants that originally grew in Sydney, such as the blue flax lily, grass trees – or the politically incorrect 'blackboys' – and mountain devil.

Along Mrs Macquarie's Bushland Walk, by Woolloomooloo Bay, horticulturists have recreated a patch of Sydney's bushland using seed and cuttings from the few small patches of remnant bush along the harbour's southern foreshores. This is the way Mrs Macquarie may have seen it in 1816 on her way to her 'Chair' at the Point.

Olympian Conservation Effort

Newington Nature Reserve, in Sydney Olympic Park *(www.sydneyolympicpark.com.au)*, is a powerful example of how Sydney can balance development and conservation. The reserve protects the eastern-most remnant of Cumberland Plain vegetation, including the endangered Sydney Turpentine-Ironbark Forest, and is a sanctuary for vulnerable native plant species and birds, mammals, reptiles and amphibians. These include a breeding colony of Red-rumped parrots and a pair of rare White-bellied sea eagles, a bird of prey with a wingspan exceeding 2m. It's also home to the endangered Green and golden bell frog, which has a distinctive three-part call that sounds like a motorbike changing gears. To get the best out of a visit keep your eyes open for birds overhead and your ears open for the sounds of native fauna.

Fungi Feast

One of Sydney's best collections of fungi can be found in Lane Cove Bushland Park, where a community of endangered *Hygrocybeae* can still be found. The colours are amazing – bright yellows, neon greens, psychedelic oranges and more. The steep slopes and rock outcrops over which water drips into leaf litter below provide ideal conditions for the fungi, inedible to us but manna to different creatures nature enlists to distribute its spores.

Trees and Plants

There is an impressive 1500 species of plants that can be found within a 150km radius of the centre of Sydney.

Prince among them is the Red waratah, which, according to Aboriginal legend, was white until a wounded pigeon went from waratah to waratah looking for her mate and turned them red with her blood. (If you poke your finger into the flower it comes out red, an enduring symbol of the pigeon's blood.) The waratah is also the State's official floral emblem.

Also look out for the Gymea lily; its deep, blood-red blooms atop tall wavering stems are spectacular show-offs throughout spring and summer. Port Jackson figs are another signature plant for the city and are often found along the water's edge.

At North Head you will find some significant plant life including broad-leaved paperbark; dry, smooth barked apple; tea tree scrub; wet Sprengelia heath and the swamp oak. Visit the northeast slopes of Middle Head to see good examples of myrtle, and the Blue Mountains for Sydney peppermint; crush the leaves of this tree with dark-grey bark to release the peppermint smell.

Another good place to experience native vegetation is Botany Bay National Park. Shrubs here include the Sydney golden wattle, whose brilliant yellow flower spikes can be seen in July and August.

But perhaps no tree has generated as much excitement as the Wollemi pine, a very peculiar and precious specimen indeed. Standing up to 40m tall, with a girth of nearly 3m, it is covered in a dark green waxy foliage and has bubbly bark. It is one of the world's oldest and rarest plants and was believed extinct until David Noble, a ranger with the National Parks and Wildlife Service, happened upon one in 1994, 200km west of Sydney in The Wollemi National Park. He was out abseiling when he noticed the unusual pine and took a fallen branch home for identification. It was described as the botanical find of the century. Wollemi is an Aboriginal word meaning "look around you, keep your eyes open and watch out".

Sotheby's auctioned the first propagated Wollemi pines, which are displayed in the gardens of Sydney's elite. You can now buy them at nurseries or online at www.wollemi pine.com. The place were they are growing naturally is a closely guarded secret.

No matter what your mood – happy, sad, angry, grateful, stressed or bored – there is one, perfect space to lose yourself in the middle of Sydney. Well, not so much a space as a series of gardens, lawns and paths: the magnificent and fecund **Royal Botanic Gardens** *(RBG; www.rbgsyd.nsw.gov.au)*.

It adjoins the 34-hectare Domain, along the edge of the central business district and the harbour, and it's fairly oozing with flora and fauna that will soothe and titillate.

According to horticulturalist Dawson Oughton, the RBG began in 1816 as a garden of the colony, growing grains, fruits and vegetables. Today it features everything from begonias, herbs, orientals, succulents and natives to orchids and roses, as well as animals like Blue-tongue lizards and Eastern water dragons. Watch overhead for a Noah's Ark supply of birds, from the Australian wood duck and Channel-billed cuckoo to the Eastern rosella, Golden whistler and wonderfully named Willy wagtail. If you're in the gardens at night, listen for the call of this little bird, which sounds like "sweet pretty creature".

With such an inventory, the Gardens appear an oasis of tranquillity and beauty. But it has come at great price, according to Edwin Wilson, author of *Poetry of Place*. "The Royal Botanic Gardens were forged through conflict – between Europeans and the Cadigal; convicts and trees; convict chain gangs and their supervisors; gardeners and the elements (poor soil, drought, disease); land-grabbers…and finally between the creators themselves, in that 200-year-long clash of egos."

Yet in that time, "battalions of the idle and the curious have loitered here with intent – the picket fence and the parade of layabouts and lovers, hoi polloi and gentry, convict, emancipist and free, pensioners and children, students, poets, ratbags, tourists and groups of family and friends – with memories of picnics, promenades, trysts, secret wishes, ice creams, trees, statues and feeding the ducks," he acknowledges.

Palm Grove, established in 1862, has one of the world's finest collections of palms, and the combination of magnificent, towering fronds populated with fruit bats is deliciously eery (see Grey-headed flying foxes, page 38).

Nature Trip

Ku-ring-gai Chase National Park *(www.nationalparks.nsw.gov.au)*, 25km north of the CBD, is a great place to see many vulnerable birds, animals and plants. As well as important plant and animal communities, it contains a many Aboriginal sites and European historic places. The park includes the land east of the Sydney–Newcastle Expressway, south of the Hawkesbury River, west of Pittwater and north of Mona Vale Rd between St Ives and Ingleside. It also comprises most of Barrenjoey Head. Established in 1894, Ku-ring-gai Chase is the second-oldest national park in Australia.

The Sydney Tropical Centre comprises two striking glasshouses where the weird and colourful heliconias attract oohs and aahs from plant fanciers. Heliconias are closely related to bananas – the shape of the leaves is quite lush and dramatic. The flowers are always brightly coloured – vibrant pinks, reds, yellows and scarlets – and striking.

The RBG features a few knock-out fountains and sculptures, like the bronze cast Venus Fountain – a statue of Venus with cupids and dolphins at her feet – in the Lower Garden. Water sprays from each of the dolphins and each of the cupids. The Levy Drinking Fountain, near the Woolloomooloo Gate, is a magnificent Art Nouveau sculpture and one of the few large public drinking fountains that still stands in the city. It was built in 1889 and features the water nymph Diana, the goddess of purity, and a red and grey granite base.

Sadly, in recent years, cuts in funding have seen the number of staff who maintain the gardens dwindle. So, before you leave the garden, go to the Wishing Tree, a Norfolk Island pine at the intersection of the two major pathways of the Middle Garden, and make a wish that the powers-that-be will realise the value of this oasis to those who dwell in the city.

The Botanic Gardens Trust also manages **Mt Annan Botanic Gardens** *(www.rbgsyd .nsw.gov.au/annan/the_garden)*, a natural wonderland that rolls over 416 hectares of hills and lakes and contains thousands of native plants. It's a good place to take those unfamiliar with some of Australia's natural assets, or to spend the afternoon catching up on some native botany yourself. The best spots include the Banksia Garden – set in a cool gully and including grevilleas, waratahs, banksias, hakeas and rainforest species – and the Cypress Pine Aboretum.

The Mount Tomah Botanic Garden in the Blue Mountains are covered on page 172.

Slow-mo ⇒ **Garden**

Brighten your summer days with the sight of local butterflies flitting through your garden by planting sweet-nectared native plants such as banksias, wattles and Sweet bursaria. Clusters of prickly native shrubs are suitable for small native birds to nest in, or you could install nesting boxes for larger species. A favourite shrub for attracting local birds is grevillea – birds love the bright orange and yellow-and-red flowers, and so do humans. It goes without saying that planting natives is best for your garden and the natural biodiversity, as these hardy plants thrive without too many demands on both the gardener and the water supply. Pester your local nursery to stock more natives, or patronise ones that already do. Mail-order site http://natives2u.com.au/ allows you to choose native plants by flower colour – great for those who don't exactly have a green-thumb knowledge.

And don't forget that your local council will often be able to give or sell you native plants through their own nursery, so check with them before you go other places. For keen gardeners, the award-winning **Sydney Wildflower Nursery West** *(Marsden Park; 9628 4448)* also stocks bush foods, jams, spices and tea, and is worth a visit.

Along with inspiring ocean vistas, we have one of the most diverse and spectacular marine environments on the planet. In 2007, around 1600 Humpback whales passed through the harbour, leaping spectacularly and occasionally treating onlookers to a bit of a party trick: swimming on their sides with a long flipper held out of the water. Up to 16m long, they have black, stocky bodies and a small dorsal fin. Look out for them in June and July, and again in October and November.

From June to August, you might be lucky enough to see the vulnerable Southern right whale as it travels north to breed. Up to 18m long, it has a black body with white patches on its head and lower jaw to which barnacles attach, and two separate blowholes. They tend to hang around as they teach their young the finer points of swimming.

And on rocky outcrops north of Sydney, there are also occasional sightings of New Zealand fur seal, which feed on fish, seabirds and sometimes unfortunate penguins. They are under threat from collisions with boats and entanglement in nets and traps, as well as oil spills.

A good place to go to see endangered and vulnerable marine life is **Cabbage Tree Bay Aquatic Reserve** *(Manly)*, which includes the whole foreshore of the bay from Manly Surf Life Saving Club to the northern end of Shelly Beach headland. Surrounded by three national parks, the reserve is home to a rare colony of Little penguins, seahorses, turtles, pelicans, cormorants and more than 550 species of fish. Look out for weedy seadragons; they are reddish-orange with purple-blue stripes, white spots and yellow markings, and resemble every child's idea of the magical seahorse. Other regular visitors include whales, seals and dolphins. Cabbage Tree Bay is not patrolled but, nevertheless, is frequently used during summer for swimming, snorkelling and diving. To see the bird species, you need only take a seat on the foreshore and be patient. The Little penguins can prove elusive, however, and with good reason, as their population has frequently been at risk from threats such as dogs.

Clovelly Bay is part of the **Bronte-Coogee Aquatic Reserve**, which takes in the whole foreshore from the southern end of Bronte Beach to the rock baths at Coogee Beach – 4km of coastline. At first glance the brutal concrete of the bay looks like a WWII submarine pen. But the profusion of fluorescent-coloured snorkels and flippers gives away the fact that this sheltered stretch of pristine water between Gordon's Bay and Bronte is teeming with protected sea life. From garfish, hardyheads, striped morwong, bream and zebra fish to electric-coloured wrasse and large green and blue gropers, this is like a pocket-sized Ned's Beach (Lord Howe Island) underwater experience. The mouth to Clovelly is protected by a breakwater, sheltering the bay and swimmers who predominantly explore closest to the entrance. A long, sandy beach at the bay's western end and an adjoining children's tidal pool provide the perfect family environment. Picnic and toilet facilities can be found along both sides of the bush-regenerated bay, with Seasalt Cafe offering good food along with uninterrupted views.

For a list of marine reserves that are good for scuba diving, coastal walks or just wandering around, see www.nswmarineparks.org.au.

Cohabitants

How our furry and feathered friends are coping with human impact depends on the species. Brushtail possums have adapted so well to urbanisation that they're now more prevalent in the city than the bush. And although Ringtail possums are gone from the central business area of Sydney, says Martyn Robinson, a naturalist at the Australian Museum, they're still common in the suburbs.

On the other hand, 146 species, nine populations and 21 ecological communities are listed as endangered or vulnerable in the Sydney metro region, among them the Little penguin and the Grey-headed flying fox.

At the home of Betty Iles, a former animal conditioner for Taronga Zoo, six **Grey-headed flying foxes** rescued from bushfire areas hang upside down in sweaters she has hung on a clothesline for them to keep warm. It's amazing to see them up close with their big, colour-receptive eyes protruding from the sleeves and necklines; and their babies tucked up into their furry chests.

In the wild, Grey-headed flying foxes congregate in large numbers at roosting sites in rainforest patches, melaleuca stands, mangroves, riparian woodland or modified vegetation in urban areas. They perform an important role as seed dispersers and long-range pollinators of hardwoods. They migrate frequently, depending on the weather and availability of food, but become attached to particular camps where young are born. Their wingspan of up to 1m and patch of golden-orange fur (like a bib around the collar) make them an impressive sight when in flight.

The best place to see them is at the Royal Botanic Gardens, where around 5000 hang around in Palm Grove, their translucent wings wrapped around them like shrouds – it's all very Gotham City. The RBG is trying to discourage the appearance of more fruit bats because they are damaging heritage-listed trees (not to mention the overriding smell of bat pee). But, if the truth be known, it is for the flying foxes that many people visit the gardens. There is also a large colony in the north shore suburb of Gordon at the Ku-ring-gai Flying-fox Reserve Habitat. Flying foxes begin leaving their camp 20 minutes after sunset to feed throughout the metropolitan area. Watch from the bridge on Rosedale Rd at Gordon (between Minns Rd and Glenview St).

The endangered **Little** or **Fairy penguin** is almost like a mythical creature – with its

'A Friend Ever True'

Waratah Park is famous as the home of Skippy the Bush Kangaroo, television's first marsupial megastar. Sectioned off from the beautiful Ku-ring-gai National Park, it was the setting for the iconic TV '60s series. Although it was closed ahead of renovations at the time of writing, Waratah Park (13 Namba Rd, Duffys Forest; www.waratahpark.com.au) remains a sanctuary for native fauna, including some of Skippy's descendants no doubt.

round, waddling body, it looks as if it has emerged from a children's book of yesteryear. Fairy penguins, weighing about 1kg and standing only 40cm tall, are the smallest in the world. The only known surviving mainland colony in NSW is in the Cabbage Tree Bay Aquatic Reserve in Manly (see page 35) where a few still remain under houses and gardens and around the shore. It's quite amazing to have such a threatened population in an iconic location so close to the centre of Australia's biggest city.

According to the Manly Environment Centre, in 1952 there were several penguin colonies in the Manly area, totalling about 500 birds. However, the majority were either shot or destroyed by dogs. In 1990 a long-term Manly resident, alarmed at Government plans to 'flog off' the foreshore, organised a campaign to save the remaining colony. Six nesting boxes were installed and a habitat restoration programme begun, including the replanting of native species, cleanups and education. In 1995 the penguins were nominated as a threatened colony and the Department of Environment and Conservation now undertakes microchipping, monitoring and protection of this rare colony. It has even trained volunteer 'Penguin Wardens' to patrol the beach during summer when the north harbour is busiest.

Still in Manly, you'll find one of the last surviving local colonies of endangered **Longnosed bandicoots** (others include the Royal, Heathcote, Ku-ring-gai Chase and Garigal National Parks). Bandicoots were abundant until the 1960s, but have been devastated by urbanisation, cars and pets. Bandicoots come out at night in search of insects, plants and fungus to eat, using their long, pointed muzzles to find their food.

Birds of Sydney

To some, the scavenging **Australian white ibis** has become a nuisance. But they distinguish Australian parks, says Martyn Robinson of the Australian Museum. "The Ibis were originally from the swamplands but, in the 1970s, some hand-raised chicks were sent to wander," he says. "Not shy of handouts, they found park environments to their liking. Then some wild ibis flew down and bred with the tame ibis, which resulted in a large population in an urban area."

With their regular breeding grounds in the Macquarie Marshes and Gwydir wetlands devastated by drought, White ibis have found refuge across the eastern seaboard, and particularly within the Sydney basin.

Another, much rarer, bird that you'll see on occasion is the **Powerful owl**. Tony Dymond, of the Cumberland Bird Observers' Club, says there are about 30 to 40 pairs of Powerful owls in the Sydney basin. At around 60cm high, they are Australia's biggest owl, and their favourite food is medium-sized mammals such as Ringtail possums and Greater gliders. They'll also occasionally take roosting birds and large beetles, as well as fruit bats. They have been spotted clutching prey in their talons outside Macquarie University, at the Australian Museum and at a law firm in North Sydney. No lawyer jokes please.

September to November is generally the best time for your own bird-spotting, advises Dymond, when "our summer migrants have arrived and most birds are busy establishing pair bonds, establishing territories and defending them, courting and starting to nest. They are at their most vocal and most active at this time of the year."

While you can see kookaburras, Sulphur-crested cockatoos and native parrots in many parts of suburban Sydney, it's worth a trip to a national park for some serious species spotting. If you've never seen a **Gang-gang cockatoo**, head to the Royal National Park near Sutherland or the Lane Cove National Park and listen for strong, stuttered, creaky growls evocative of a rusty hinge. This relatively small, dark-grey cockatoo is listed as endangered. You may also find them in the Ku-ring-gai and Hornsby areas.

"Go to Centennial Park in Paddington to see cormorants, Dusky moorhens, Musk duck and Eurasia coot," says Dymond. "It's best to pack a picnic, sit on the grasses near the ponds, and let these birds come to you."

At Cumberland State Forest, at West Pennant Hills, there are nine species of parrot, as well as the Powerful owl, Southern boobook, Eastern whipbird and Satin bowerbird. The last is related to birds of paradise and nests 4m to 5m up in trees. "The male builds a bower," says Dymond, "where he does courtship and decorates it with blue pegs, blue straws, or anything blue he can find."

At Sydney's northern beaches, like Long Reef, there are wading and sea birds aplenty. The Sooty oystercatcher is an unmistakable, large wader, with a bright orange-red bill and pink legs and feet. It gives a loud whistling call before it takes flight. The tiny Red-necked stints breed in Siberia and migrate to Australia for our summer. They're best observed at high tide, when they are normally roosting.

The **Cumberland Bird Observers' Club** (*www.cboc.org.au; 9639 8549*) conducts at least 40 bird-watching trips every year all over the greater Sydney region. All are welcome; no bookings required. ∎

Be

SLOW WITHOUT EFFORT

SEE
Sites for Sore Eyes

- · -

" THE GREATEST THING A HUMAN SOUL EVER DOES IN
THIS WORLD IS TO SEE SOMETHING...TO SEE CLEARLY IS
POETRY, PROPHECY AND RELIGION ALL IN ONE. "

John Ruskin, *Modern Painters*

S ight is the most obvious sense of all. It dominates our experience of our surrounds: tells us if something is smooth, beautiful, hard, colourful or fresh. It's also the most stimulated sense, and so the first to fade into the background of our attention. Just because our eyes are open doesn't mean we're noticing, looking or glimpsing microscopic versions of universal truths. Watch the cycle of life in a single leaf cringing on a twig, crumpling up and, finally, letting go. Don't think there's nothing to see in the dark – imagine the earth turning away from the sun to face the gawping reaches of far-flung galaxies. How you see the world is shaped by your own perception; change that and the world will change with you.

What's That?

It's easy to pass the same building or monument every day without noticing it or wondering why it's there. Or to walk down a city street with eyes planted at ground level. Look up, observe your surrounds; you're in for a few surprises.

Part of having a slow approach to life is taking the time to notice your surroundings. You've probably passed some of these buildings, monuments and structures (some of which are virtually unmissable) hundreds of times but, in the rush from A to B, haven't stopped to think what they might be, why they're there or whose big idea they were in the first place.

There's a touch of Egypt in the **obelisk** *(Bathurst and Elizabeth Sts)* sitting on the edge of Hyde Park. But don't be fooled, there's nothing Nile-like in this particular structure, even if it does incorporate sphinxes. George Thornton had it built in 1857 when he was mayor of Sydney. At the time, locals called it 'Thornton's Scent Bottle'. You guessed it, it's a sewer vent.

The **table in the wall** *(Hyde Park Barracks)* is a poignant memorial to the Great Irish Famine and commemorates the 4200 women processed here when the Barracks was the Immigrant Women's Depot and Asylum (1848–86). The memorial was designed by Adelaide artists Hossein and Angela Valamanesh, and built in 1998. On the internal side of the wall, which represents Australia, the long table is slightly institutional-looking, with plate and spoon and a place to sit. There are also a couple of books and a sewing basket. On the outside of the wall, signifying Ireland, the table's much smaller – sitting on it is a hollow bowl, which can't hold anything, plus a few shriveled potatoes and a shovel.

The mad-looking **castle at Castle Cove**, on the headland across from Castlecrag and Middle Cove, was built by Henry Hastings Willis, a member of the first Commonwealth Parliament. Although it may look like a ring-in from somewhere else, with its corner turrets, battlements and three-storey tower, there are nationalistic elements to its design. The stained glass, for instance, has designs of waratahs and Christmas bells, and the plaster ceiling rosettes incorporate native plants. It's called Innisfallen, after Innisfallen Abbey in Ireland, and it stayed in the Willis family until 1988.

The **P&O fountain** *(cnr Hunter and Castlereagh Sts)* would have to be the only fountain in the world to be a major player in an obscenity case. No one remembers that sculptor Tom Bass designed it in 1963; they're far more interested in the *Oz* magazine obscenity trial. The *Oz* editors, Richard Neville, Richard Walsh and Martin Sharp, were photographed for the February 1964 cover of the satirical magazine using the fountain as a urinal, with the blurb stating: "This is no ordinary urinal. It has a continual flushing system and basins handily set at different standing heights." The judge claimed

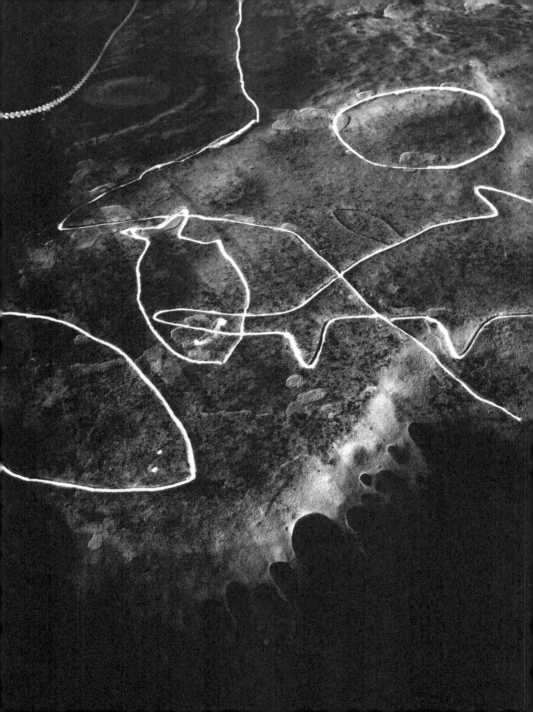

it would encourage "public pissing" and sentenced Walsh and Neville to six months in prison, Sharp to four. The sentences were overturned on appeal after a huge public outcry and, yes, the fountain is occasionally used as a toilet.

With its intricate exterior detailing and elegant design, you could be forgiven for thinking that **strange-looking building** on Small St, off Willoughby Rd, was a church or gallery. But no, the 1930s building is one of 13 incinerators Walter Burley Griffin and business partner Eric Nicholls designed in Sydney. Their idea was that industrial buildings didn't need to be ugly and, if they were built in a residential area, they should fit into their surroundings. It's heritage listed, and stopped operating as an incinerator in 1967. For a few years it ran as a restaurant (char grilled, anyone?) and was converted to offices in 1989. Most of the Burley Griffin incinerators have been demolished, although there is one other in Glebe.

Heading up William St, it's impossible to miss the **Coca Cola sign** marking the entrance to Kings Cross. It's the biggest billboard in the southern hemisphere, and is in two parts. The left side is 20m by 12m, and internally lit by 1000 fluorescent lamps. The more famous animated section on the right consists of 88 bars of red tubing, hidden behind reflectors, and 800 fluorescent lamps projecting 13 different patterns, all operated by a computer. Now you know.

As your train pulls into Central Station, you can't help wondering about the **golfer on the roof** of Sharpies Golf Store, who's been putting Tiger Woods to shame since 1958. He might be looking a bit worse for wear these days, and is currently looking for a new home, but he had been hitting a hole-in-one every 20 seconds or so for almost half a century – if you do the maths, that adds up to about 75 million of them over the years.

You can walk down George St every day and never really think about what's going on above street level. The **Dymocks building** (right next door to the shop) is one place that warrants a closer look – it's a 1930s heritage building, for a start, and holds over 100 businesses and shops. Getting in and out of the lift at random can yield a whole load of surprises: Reiki masters, hearing-aid specialists and bridal boutiques are neighbours with antique jewellers, a fishing tackle shop, make-up college and Italian language institute. It's a complete treasure trove, with a healthy dag quotient.

" **I JUST WENT DOWN TO GET A CUP OF TEA, I THINK, AND FOUND THIS LOVELY RESTAURANT. IT WAS A GREAT SURPRISE TO ME. I WAS STRUCK BY ITS COLOUR AND GENERAL DESIGN...SCARLET, GREEN AND WHITE HELD ME SPELLBOUND. I QUICKLY BEGAN DRAWING, WRITING THE COLOUR IN WORDS AS I WORKED.** **"**

Grace Cossington Smith talking about the creation of her painting *The Lacquer* Room
(c. 1935) – a favourite at the Art Gallery of NSW.

Slow Architecture

There are many different ways you could describe a building as slow, from the fact that it is mindful of the environment or because it's almost handmade. Sydney architect Peter Stutchbury believes there's a slowness to "places that attempt to capture the ingredients of where they are. Those ingredients could be anything from climate to people to barking dogs."

Stutchbury's houses are beautifully crafted from modest materials, many of them located on the northern beaches. "When you actually place yourself in a position that you're making a veil to where you are – there has to be a sensitivity that comes out of that that draws twice upon your senses," he says. "It's that 'twiceness', that secondary look at things that's most important, that brings you to a certain awareness of other things going on, or the patterns or makeup of the place.

"Coogee Baths are amazing," says Peter. "It's the site and the structure: the way the timber structure is carefully situated on the edge of the country, on the edge of Australia. It's their proportion, their scale in the position, their elevation over the water. Those key things give them that slowness, that quality of repose.

"In a funny way, the buildings on Barrenjoey Headland qualify [as slow] too," says Peter. "The lighthouse-keeper's houses are cut into the hill for weather protection. They have a very particular sense of human protection or safety that allows you to retreat to a space that's totally private and inward-looking, or move to the other side of a building which is completely exposed and open."

AAA Tour

Walking, by its very nature, is a slow activity. But a walk can swing from a dawdle to a sprint when you're with the enthusiastic figure of architect Ben Gerstel, who's keen to show you around the architecturally rich suburb of Castlecrag, where he lives.

Around a dozen of us meet on a Saturday afternoon at Castlecrag shops on Edinburgh Rd. Before the Australian Architecture Association (AAA) tour starts, Ben chats to some locals who say they won't be home this afternoon, but we must head down their driveway and have a good look at their award-winning Stanic Harding house, designed in 2001.

Even longtime Sydneysiders need a guide in Castlecrag. It was planned by Walter Burley Griffin (who designed Canberra), but the word 'planned' gives the wrong impression – there's nothing ordered or predictable about Castlecrag. The bush-covered peninsula is made up little laneways and tiny hillside reserves that, with their large boulders and overgrown vegetation, have more than a whiff of *Picnic at Hanging Rock* about them. It makes all the difference to have an expert on hand to guide you through the area and its history.

We hear not only about the hospital built for a member of the first federal parliament, King O'Malley, but also about Marcia Hathaway, the last person to die as a result of a shark attack in Sydney Harbour, in 1963. From the street, we look at dozens of houses: from ones designed by Burley Griffin and some of the

design classics of the 50s and 60s to the area's newest additions. As we walk past a Burley Griffin house undergoing a major restoration, the owners invite us in and give us a very personal tour of the project, detailing all the stumbling blocks they've encountered along the way, as well as showing us the meticulous work they're doing to restore the house to original. That's the beauty of an AAA tour – you can expect the unexpected.

AAA *(www.architecture.org.au)* holds dozens of tours throughout the year in Sydney and beyond – some walking, others by bus or boat.

Colours of Sydney

Red post boxes are on virtually every street corner. Use them to send postcards to your friends, even ones you see every few days. Think what a thrill it'll give them when they open their mailbox – much more exciting than junk mail.

Yellow is the name of a cafe/restaurant on Macleay St, Potts Point. Housed in what was once the Yellow House (named after Van Gogh's studio), it was the centre of bohemian Sydney from the 50s to the early 70s. It's where artists such as Martin Sharp, Brett Whiteley, Peter Kingston and George Gittoes covered every surface with their artworks; where Peter Weir screened his early films; Ellis D Fogg ran his psychedelic lightshows and Little Nell danced the floorboards. Before they came along, it had been home to a number of artists, including Russell Drysdale, and the site of the Terry Clune Galleries, which exhibited Sydney's emerging artists of the time, including John Olsen, Robert Hughes and Robert Klippel. The exterior paint colour, an exact match of the shade used during its colourful past, sings in a neighbourhood more accustomed to the quietly discreet.

Green is the colour of the future, now that we're all more eco-aware. Visit the Eco-Logic exhibition in the **Powerhouse Museum** *(www.powerhousemuseum.com)* and, through displays ranging from worm farming to saving water, find out how to create a more sustainable lifestyle. If you're a student, get together with a few friends and book a tour of Michael Mobbs' and Heather Armstrong's sustainable house (www.sustainablehouse .com.au) in Chippendale. They've been living in it since 1996, using only rainwater and solar energy, and processing all wastewater on site. If you can't do the tour, read the book *Sustainable House*.

Blue is surfeit in Sydney, displaying more hues, tones and shades of blue than you could name. From the bluey-mauve drift of jacaranda in springtime (the blossoms make brilliant witches hats for little fingers, as every kid knows) to the blue notes from the few remaining places to hear jazz around town. ∎

> **" IT'S A SUNSET CITY. THE TALL BUILDINGS ARE SILHOUETTES IN THE FAMILIAR SHAPES I KNOW AND LOVE SO MUCH, AND WHEN I GET AN ANGLE ON THE FARTHER SHORE OF THE HARBOUR, BITS AND POINTS OF LIGHT ARE PICKED OUT BY THE SUN, AND ONE BY ONE, AND OFTEN SEVERAL AT A TIME, WINDOWS CATCH THE SUN AND THROW A BLINDING REFLECTION RIGHT IN MY FACE AND I HAVE TO TURN AWAY, DAZZLED. "**

David Ireland, *City of Women*, a novel set around Darlinghurst.

Best Place to See...

Early Sydney is on show at the Conservatorium of Music *(Macquarie St)*. During restoration works in the late 90s, on what was built in 1821 as the government stables, all sorts of archaeological remnants were unearthed. Parts of very early roads, gutters and a cistern dating back to 1790 are incorporated, in situ, into the new building and encased in glass. There are also display cases of crockery and other artefacts uncovered during the excavation.

The Queen Victoria Building looks stunning from the restaurant upstairs in the Hilton across the road. You get a spectacular front-on view of the stained glass, a hint of those exotic domes and can forget that fashion chains inhabit the place.

The Harbour Bridge seems to pop up when you least expect it. You can be driving in the suburbs and suddenly get a glimpse of it, or walking down a city street and there it will be – filling up the skyline and seeming to span the buildings on either side of the road. But the most dramatic view of it is from the Wharf Restaurant *(Pier 4/5, Hickson Rd)*. It's pretty well right there, on top of you, and you can almost feel the trains rattling overhead. It's worth it for the walk down the length of the wharf,

too, which has to be one of the best walks in Sydney. The gorgeous old timber wharf was restored in the most subtle and sensitive way (winning the state's top architectural award), with most of the structure of the building exposed and celebrated. The walls of the simple but surprisingly grand structure are now lined with hundreds of posters for the plays that have been presented there over the past 20 years or so, and those are definitely worth a look as well *(www.sydneytheatre.com.au)*.

The city assumes a holiday feel when observed from the No 324 bus route, which starts at Circular Quay, goes through the Cross, then along New South Head Rd through Double Bay, Rose Bay and then heads up the hill towards Vaucluse. It's around Kincoppal (the school with probably the best view in the world) that you'll look over the harbour and back towards the city. It's a priceless view for the price of a bus fare.

The ocean is confronting (in a good way) from the park bench on the headland at Turrametta Beach park near Warriewood. It looks straight out towards the horizon and you suddenly realise that, yes, you are sitting right on the edge of a continent.

Bridges

A city that makes so much mileage (and quite rightly so) out of its harbour is sure to have some pretty impressive bridges. It's easy, though, as you're going about your daily commute, to either not notice them or curse them because of their bottlenecks. When next stuck in a traffic jam, consider what's actually holding you up.

Sydney Harbour Bridge

Tom Ugly's Bridge

You might already have a fair idea of what the **Sydney Harbour Bridge** looks like, and given the hoo-hah over its 75th anniversary, we probably don't need to tell you much about it. But one of our favourite things is how long it took to build. Government architect Francis Greenway (whose buildings include Hyde Park Barracks and Macquarie Lighthouse) first suggested a bridge from Dawes Point to the North Shore…and that was in 1815. It wasn't until 1922 that legislation was passed for its construction – we know governments work slowly, but that's ridiculous.

And we have to put in a plug for the one with the best name, **Tom Ugly's Bridge**, built in the 20s across the Georges River. As for the ugly bit of it, there are several theories – an Aborigine of that name lived nearby in a cave, or it might have been named after Tom Illigley, a local fisherman, or Tom Huxley, a caretaker on a large estate. All, one would assume, aesthetically challenged.

Gladesville Bridge

One of the best views of the harbour has to be from the **Gladesville Bridge**. You're so high up you feel as if you're flying, with all the bays laid out in front of you and the city in the distance. When built in the '60s, it was the longest single-span, concrete arch bridge in the world. Gladesville is named after the convict John Glade, who arrived here in 1791, did incredibly well and ended up owning great swathes of land in the area. The suburb didn't take off until the middle of the 19th century when the land was subdivided and advertised as being suitable for 'gentlemen's residences'.

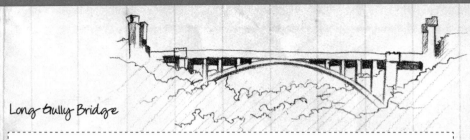

Long Gully Bridge

Not far from the Harbour Bridge is one of our most spectacular spans, the **Long Gully Bridge**, marking the entrance to Northbridge. The bizarre, castle-looking structure was built in two stages – the 1890s and the 1930s. The first, which had towers like the ones there now, was built to open up the area for housing and was considered an engineering wonder. It became a tourist attraction and people paid to cross it. When housing development didn't go so well, the bridge fell into disrepair and had to be rebuilt. The sandstone towers were retained, but the roadway openings were increased and walkways cut through.

Ashfield's Battle Bridge

Along Parramatta Rd, one of Sydney's least prepossessing thoroughfares, you'll find **Ashfield's Battle Bridge**, a stone arch with the decidedly unglamorous job of crossing a stormwater channel. Its original 1870s arch is still intact, although hard to make out with the 1930s additions. No one's certain how Battle Creek got its name – it's either because of a convict riot during the construction of the very first bridge on the site, or because it was the venue for early prize fights.

Iron Cove Bridge

On the other side of the harbour, the heritage-listed Art Deco–style **Iron Cove Bridge** was designed in 1942 and opened in 1955 by the premier and colonial treasurer JJ Cahill (yes, the one of Cahill Expressway fame). It replaced a wrought-iron bridge from the 1880s, remnants of which are visible on both sides of the cove, just south of the current bridge.

Art

Geographically, it doesn't sound possible but you can get gorgeous views of the Heads, Bondi Beach and Cremorne from the Domain. Step into the Art Gallery of NSW *(www.artgallery.nsw.gov.au)*, and you'll witness the changing landscape of the city, from the perspective of Arthur Streeton, Margaret Preston, Grace Cossington Smith and Brett Whiteley, among others. All have created their own personal visions of the city, which have become etched into our psyches.

You can almost feel the heat and sand in that most iconic image, Max Dupain's *Sunbaker*, the black-and-white photo of a Sydneysider on the beach. Brett Whiteley's slightly warped harbour views, with their intense colours and odd perspective, throw a unique light on familiar surrounds. For more Whiteley, and to get a sense of where he lived and worked, take a weekend trip to Brett Whiteley's Studio *(2 Raper St, Surry Hills)*. Tucked down an alleyway and behind a nondescript front door (albeit with the artist's sculpture attached to the front wall), the warehouse is a wonderful insight into his world. It's all there: sketchbooks, reference books, record collection, postcards and unfinished paintings. There are changing exhibitions of Whiteley's work and a small shop.

The State Library *(www.sl.nsw.gov.au)* is always showing off its uniquely broad art collection relating to Sydney. The library also has a fantastic collection of digital art prints available to purchase (http://shop.atmitchell.com/).

Another place you may not readily associate with art is Manly, but Manly Art Gallery *(West Esplanade)*, a couple of minutes' walk from the ferry, past the harbour pool, is a little gem. Its collection of local artworks includes Tom Roberts' *The Flower Sellers*, Lloyd Rees' *The Barn* (both stolen in 1976, but returned several years later) and Ethel Carrick Fox's *Manly Beach – Summer is Here*. There are also thousands of historic photographs of the northern beaches and 89 objects on permanent loan from the David Jones' collection, including men's and women's bathing costumes, beachwear and accessories.

To see the spirit of this age in art, get on the mailing list of galleries to stay abreast of what's happening. Our artist-run gallery of choice is China Heights *(Level 3, 16-28 Foster St, Surry Hills; www.chinaheights.com)*, upstairs and under a kung-fu studio, in a run down and character-filled Surry Hills building; it's only open on weekends and, a bonus for those with a short attention span, a new exhibition opens every Friday night.

Things that
caught my eye...

HEAR
Listen to Sydney

- • -

" DON'T UNDERESTIMATE THE VALUE OF DOING NOTHING,
OF JUST GOING ALONG,
LISTENING TO ALL THE THINGS YOU CAN'T HEAR,
AND NOT BOTHERING. "

Winnie the Pooh

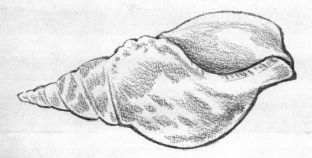

see

hear

smell

taste

touch

S ound acts as a map to our surrounds. Particular noises, or the total lack of noise, not only locates us in a place but also stirs the emotions. Whether conscious of it or not, sound rolls like waves to our ears – a fitting analogy for a city synchronised with the sea. Sounds trigger involuntary reactions: a clenched jaw from an unanswered car alarm, or goose pimples from a euphoric symphony performance. Sydney's soundscape has distinct rhythms, orchestrated by its unique geography and social structures. They set Sydney apart from anywhere else, and distinguish morning from night, weekday from weekend, and decade from decade.

A Schedule of Sound

The sound of Sydney was once epitomised by Speaker's Corner in the Domain. In the 1870s this spot was designated "the heart of democracy in Sydney". For more than 100 years, Sunday afternoons were characterised by rants and raves about religion, politics and nudity, even dried fruit and nuts. Modern technology has altered the timbre of public debate. Why get on a soapbox when you blog for a worldwide audience or text message from wherever you happen to be? Ironically, it's getting harder to sound out the city over the ringtones, bleeps and buzzes unless we consciously zoom into Sydney's more enjoyable wavelengths. So, listen up.

The muted crescendo of waves passing overhead while you're submerged in the sea is quentessentially **January**. Breaking to the surface brings the piercing screech of a lifesaver's whistle, as the disobedient swim outside the flags. For those who'd rather give rips, rolling surf and crowds a miss, there's the far gentler Redleaf Pool on the harbour at Double Bay. It's away from the masses and quiet enough that, when the wind's blowing in the right direction, you can float on your back and hear the lions roaring in Taronga Park Zoo.

The swish of ducks landing on water is an aural treat at any time, but is most common in summer when inland areas dry up and squadrons of ducks flock to the lake in Centennial Park and Sydney's other wetlands (see www.livingharbour.net/birds for a map). Other evocative summer sounds include the thwack of cricket balls on wood at suburban ovals or the beach, and the laconic drone of the commentators on TV and radio.

The extreme heat of **February** brings the cracking of bark stripping from stringybark trees and falling through the foliage. These tatty-looking gum trees are found dotted around, including places like the Sun Valley Cabbage Gum Forest between Warimoo and Valley Heights in the Blue Mountains. The elementary crunching of bark underfoot easily trumps the pleasure that people from milder climes get from standing on their dried leaves.

It's also the time for tropical storms – the growling of thunder and sharp cracks of lightning. In the preceding stillness, listen for the increasingly hysterical bush telegraph as word goes around the bird world that it's time to find shelter. And afterwards, the discordant chorus of insects and birds as they make the most of the newly drenched surrounds.

On a warm summer evening, on the northern end of the Harbour Bridge, the rattling of trains overhead mixes with the screams from masochists scaring themselves silly on the Wild Mouse at Luna Park, the heritage-listed amusement park that opened its doors (or should we say 'mouth') in 1935.

In **March**, you can't miss the tut-tutting of critics, with the announcement of who won the Archibald Prize and the inevitable debate about the nature of portraiture: is it about establishing a realistic representation or revealing the sitter's character? The country's most well-known portrait prize is held annually (since 1921) at the Art Gallery of NSW.

For a buzz of a different type, hear the roaring motors of the dykes on bikes as they cover the Sydney Gay & Lesbian Mardi Gras course on two wheels, drowning out the dance beat from floats in their wake.

April is a time for quiet reflection, as the Last Post sounds at Martin Place on Anzac Day. The bugle call traditionally marked the phases of a day in military service: the Last Post heralding the day's end. It's trumpeted at the dawn service as a final farewell – symbolising an end to the duties of those who died at war. And is followed by a minute or two of silence.

There's something about **May**, as we head towards winter, that makes us notice *Big Issue* vendors braving the elements. Hear Rob's hypnotic jingle down at Circular Quay, or have a chat with cheery John on Castlereagh St.

As the weather gets colder and the nights draw in, head indoors to listen to the Australian Brandenburg Orchestra (www.brandenburg.com.au) playing at City Recital Hall, Angel Place. In a space with brilliant acoustics, you'll hear baroque works played on period instruments. That includes violins with gut strings and, no, it's not cat but sheep gut. The slang term derives from bygone audiences taunting that the strings sounded like the screeches of a disemboweled tabby. They obviously weren't listening to these guys.

Early mornings in **June** are punctuated by foghorns on the harbour (a sure sign that winter's finally arrived), and are a time when museums seem particularly appealing. The Museum of Sydney (cnr Phillip and Bridge Sts; www.hht.net.au/museums) has tales about all aspects of Sydney life in its audiovisual displays, but the Justice & Police Museum (cnr Albert and Phillip Sts; www.hht.net.au/museums), only open on weekends (except in January), has an intriguing oral history component to its exhibitions – and there's nothing like a good crime story to fire the imagination.

On a winter evening, the reverent clang of church bells can transport the city to another world and another time. Thursday is practice night for the bellringers of St Mary's Cathedral (St Mary's Rd) who create glorious music on the 14 bells, the biggest of which weighs a massive 1741kg (about the weight of your average caravan). The bellringers do it all from a room below the tower, so they won't be deafened by the vibrations. The bells of St Mary's Cathedral first rang out on New Year's Day 1844, and, today, chime during services (10am Sunday and noon Wednesday).

Primal sounds of males engaged in battle fill the air of virtually every Sydney suburban oval in **July**, as everyone from the tiniest tots to grown men throw or kick balls in the pursuit of various football codes. The primal sounds also emanate from the sidelines as over-excited parents, partners and other sports nuts voice their disapproval or delight.

The State Library of NSW (www.sl.nsw.gov.au) makes a magnificent mid-winter retreat. It's easy to find something to spark your imagination (leafing through 50-year-old Sydney newspapers is particularly entertaining), but the 1910 Mitchell Library is irresistible when you're in desperate need for a bit of peace. The slightest noise echoes around the large chamber, stairways and walkways, which are lined with floor-to-ceiling books. There's a gentle hum of activity and the reassuring scrunch of footsteps on lino.

The northern hemisphere summer signals a major southbound migration in **August,** as you'll discover listening to the different European languages on the No 380 bus to Bondi. Rug up for an invigorating walk along the beach, among the squalls and squawks. Early-morning weekend walks along the Parramatta River and other reaches of the harbour are accompanied by the mesmerising slap of oars on water as hardy rowers train.

The start of spring in **September** is a special enough occasion to savour the gentle drone of the flying boat (www.seaplanes.com.au), and book a trip from Rose Bay to Whale Beach or Cottage Point where you're almost guaranteed

when accompanied by the native birds they attract. She-oaks, which need breeze for pollination, are found at North Head and Ball's Head particularly.

November, before the heat of summer hits, is the perfect time to savour the city's quieter sounds. Head to the natural amphitheatre at Nielsen Park, where you'll find a whisper from one side can be heard loud and clear on the other. Much louder are the sounds coming from the Woolloomooloo docks when the navy hits town and it's strike-up-the-band time with '76 Trombones' and other old favourites.

December is heralded by Christmas carols, festive muzak (if we hear 'Silent Night' one

·

66 OXFORD ST LAPPED THEM ROUND WITH PROMISES, LURED
THEM WITH IMPOSSIBLE DREAMS...THE WHIRL OF LIGHTS, **99**
THE PURR OF CARS, THE DISTANT, VELVETY ROAR OF THE
CITY, HALOED WITH GOLD.

From *Bobbin Up* by Dorothy Hewett

·

to be greeted by the cackles of kookaburras. We give the thumbs-up to any plane trip that starts with the slapping of waves on a seawall rather than muzak, and there's something quaintly old fashioned about the pilot pointing out landmarks along the way. Rose Bay has been the flying boat base for decades – it used to run a regular service to Lord Howe Island, until the island got its own airstrip in 1974.

The sound of breeze rustling leaves is something to behold anywhere, but the slow whistle of **October** winds rushing through the long, spindly bristles of she-oaks is strictly our own, and one that can be as noisy as semi-trailers on an open highway. They sound especially good

more time in the supermarket...) and, all through the suburbs, the ringing of cicadas. They're the loudest insects around. The Green Grocer, one of the most common species in Sydney, can produce a call in excess of 120 decibels, which is just about enough to make your ears hurt at close range.

And talking of deafening, at 1pm on Boxing Day, a cannon blasts, reverberating around South Head to signal, as it has done since 1945, the start of the Sydney to Hobart Yacht Race. And even though it's meant to be sunny at this time of year, you can almost hear the southerly bluster start to build, just to make sure the race is no cruise.

Slow-mo

Hear, Here

- Sing, even if you're not fond of the sound of your own voice.

- Close your ears and listen to your heartbeat, the whooshing of your blood or stomach gurgling.

- Put your ear to the sand and listen for the sea: sound vibrations travel 10 times faster through the ground.

- Hum with your mouth closed: it's like a massage from the inside.

- Make a compilation CD for a friend.

Mister Violin

"I'd better get the violin off the line, it looks as if it's about to rain." Harry Vatiliotis has been making stringed instruments since 1953, soon after he arrived in Australia from Cyprus. He unpegs the partly finished violin, honey-coloured with its first coating of linseed oil, and props it up in the living room of his house in Concord. Beside it are two finished instruments, ready to be collected by their new owners, one a member of a professional string quartet. In his workshop, alongside the living room, two newly made viola fronts are on the bench, and raw slabs of spruce and European maple are stacked on the floor. "The timber comes from Germany – it's what's traditionally used in violin making," Harry says. A row of hand tools, some made by Harry himself, is lined up on a shelf, a couple of power tools sit under the window, ABC Classic FM plays on the radio.

The waiting list for Harry's violins and violas, each of which takes six weeks to make, has 20 or more names on it; some are professional musicians, others keen amateurs. He's just given up making cellos and double basses, which take an enormous amount of physical effort: "I'd rather stick with the smaller ones."

Harry, who learnt his skills under Australia's foremost violin maker, AE Smith, describes himself as "a good listener". He doesn't play the violin. "I have no talent for music, which is a good thing – if I could play, that's what I'd be doing all day and I'd never get around to making the violins," he says.

His disconcertingly dismissive approach to the mystery surrounding violin-making is appealing: "You just need to make them light and strong enough so they don't collapse, and then you'll get a good sound."

He likes to hear people play before he makes their instrument, so he can adjust the design slightly depending on whether "they hack away at it or pussyfoot around". His violins can be heard in major Australian orchestras, including the Australian Opera and Ballet Orchestra, and a couple have been played by Australian musicians in an Italian opera orchestra and UK's Hallé Orchestra. "Mine produce more sound than a lot of other violins," says Harry, trying to explain the demand for them, "and they're probably better, but I'll leave that for other people to say".

Staged Sounds

With an opera house as its emblem, you'd expect Sydney to produce some unique sounds. Step up Midnight Oil, Inxs and the Necks, and let's pretend clangers like Russell Crowe's Ordinary Fear of God never happened. Among the venues valiantly keeping the scene humming, the **Vanguard** (*42 King St, Newtown*) hosts jazz, blues and roots and the venerable Basement (see page 200) has been turning it on and up for over 30 years.

Elsewhere across town, the Guinness flows and plates of bangers and mash fly out of the kitchen at the **Harp** (*900 Princes Hwy, Tempe*) where, on a good night, you'll hear top international names in Irish music, itself having put down roots in the harbour city. For a taste of gypsy music, not to mention goulash, there's always the **Double Bay Woodfire Cabaret Restaurant** (*459-465 New South Head Rd*), one of the most fabulously old-fashioned joints in town.

A Friday-night session at **Eastside Arts of Cafe Carnivale** (*Oxford St, Paddington; www.mva.org.au*) might have you believing you are in Copacabana. The band's foot-tapping, body-swaying rhythms, impromptu percussion and rich mix of European, African and Indian sounds, with a touch of '40s-nightclub thrown in, adds an exotic edge to the venue – a hall behind the Uniting Church. A surprising offshoot of the Sydney Olympics, it was originally founded as a concert platform for Sydney musicians of non-English-speaking backgrounds to perform.

At the other end of the spectrum, the Sydney Opera House is a favourite on performers' maps, even if the acoustics in the Concert Hall leave a little to be desired. But you don't have to worry about that if you check out what's on at the **Studio** (*www.sydneyoperahouse.com*), an intimate little space that often has weird and way-out music that attracts a totally different crowd from that heading off to the symphony or opera.

And just up the road, in the converted stables otherwise known as the **Conservatorium** (*www.music.usyd.edu.au*), you'll find an equally fabulous mix – jazz one night, avant garde percussion the next, followed by a Beethoven string quartet. ∎

A Sound Signal

One particular Sydney innovation conducts a syncopated flow of human traffic. The ATPD (audio-tactile pedestrian detector), developed in Sydney, sounds that it's safe for pedestrians to cross the road. Initiated in 1967 by Cecil McIlwraith, himself blind, the big, blue vibrating device, with the arrow and oversized button, now beeps at thousands of intersections around Australia, the USA and Singapore.

WHAT'S THE QUIETEST THING YOU CAN HEAR RIGHT NOW?

Some of my favorite sounds are...

SMELL
Scents and Local Sensibility

---•---

> HIT A TRIPWIRE OF SMELL
> AND MEMORIES EXPLODE ALL AT ONCE.
> A COMPLEX VISION LEAPS OUT OF THE UNDERGROWTH.

Diane Ackerman, *A Natural History of the Senses*

Smell is the most elusive and curious of senses. Ignited with every breath, it has a long and accurate memory that anchors us with a sense of place and belonging. Just a hint of something in the air can instantly transport us back to a childhood holiday and evoke the carefree feeling of a particular week.

Taken for granted and so little understood, the sense of smell works on many different levels. Much of the taste of food depends on smell. We can reject a potential partner because their scent isn't quite right, feel queasy from a waft of a food that once made us ill, and smell danger, such as smoke signifying there's fire.

Breath Sydney in deeply and you'll not only make the most of what's around you in the most profound way, but you'll find it also work wonders for your health.

Seasonal Scents

Sydney has many distinct and shifting aromas. After a trip away, the fizz of salt in the air tells us we're back in our harbour-side home; around Petersham and Dulwich Hill you'll find the irresistible smell of Portuguese and Brazilian char-grills, while Auburn's fragrance has to be the heady aroma of *simit* (ring-shaped pastries) at the Turkish bakeries. Many of Sydney's signature scents can be savoured year-round, while others are seasonal and fleeting, instinctively tying us to time and place.

January is when we really have time to take things slowly and break from routine. Go for a morning walk, and stop and smell every frangipani. Its bright, tropical scent more than makes up for its lack of good looks – one of the quintessentially Sydney sensuous experiences. Take an early evening trip to the beach and beat the queues at the fish and chip shop. Sit on the sea wall, break open that knee-burning hot package and breathe in those deliciously unhealthy smells.

The dusty smell of smoke also characterises January, as somewhere is ravaged by bushfire and a brown pall floats over the city. But take comfort from the fact that heat and smoke from fire help some native seeds germinate – part of the bush's natural regeneration cycle.

The dripping heat of **February** has its own intense scent. Backyards and balconies are warm-weather kitchens – the aroma of sizzling steaks, sausages and onions casts a mouthwatering cloud over neighbourhoods.

The weather brings out the eucalyptus haze from the bush (including the last remaining pocket of Blue Gum High Forest at St Ives). Over the Blue Mountains we can actually 'see' the comforting Vicks-like smell as that familiar smudgy mist hovering in the west.

When you live in an international destination, it's easy to become blasé about anything with even a vague whiff of tourism. But it can be fun, especially during temperate **March**, to smell Sydney through an outsider's perspective – to get a smell of the post-performance pheromones, to check out the stars' dressing rooms and to find out how small that orchestra pit really is, book into one of the Opera House backstage tours (www.sydneyoperahouse.com).

The football season gets into full swing in **April** and our favourite sporting smells return; whether it's the stimulating vapours of liniment from players as they emerge from the race, the leather of a Steeden or damp boots and wet grass as the kids come in from training.

Those in-between months, like **May**, are best for getting out and about in the evening, when a brisk walk is invigorating but not too cold that you wouldn't rather stay at home with a book and a nourishing bowl of soup.

By **June**, as winter starts to nip at the air, there's no more welcome aroma than that created by espresso machines being cranked up all over the city. It's also a good time to explore unfamiliar areas (timing it so lunch

is part of your itinerary) – that could be Lakemba, with the aromatic aqueous scent of rosewater in its cake shops, or Auburn, where you'll come across the mouthwatering smells of *icli kofte* (stuffed meatballs) and other Turkish delights (not to mention the sweet scents coming from the actual Turkish-delight factory).

Thank goodness for wattles in **July**. There's an official Wattle Day in September, when everyone is encouraged to wear green and gold, but we'll celebrate them now instead, when the rest of the bush has slowed down and the wattles are putting on a show. The aptly named sweet-scented wattle is found all over the bush, including Lane Cove National Park and the suburbs along the Cooks River.

Another olfactory revelation this month is the endangered orchid in the Tropical Centre at the Royal Botanic Gardens (RBG), called the stinky plant. The odour from the maroon, spike-shaped flowers is intense, pungent and, for some people, nauseating. To help the plant pollinate, nature designed the aroma to attract flies and carrion beetles, so you can imagine what it smells like (and perhaps why it's so rare). In fact, when the plant was originally collected in 1968 in New Guinea, the smell was so offensive that the collector threw up before making his way back up a cliff face with some flowers he'd snapped off.

For something a little more savoury, head to the RBG's Herb Garden and fill your head with smells like minty pennyroyal, pungent horseradish and soothing lavender, which grow alongside pretty paved pathways.

For an experience that manages to combine tranquility, invigoration and the smell of incense in one hit, visit some of the temples in the Fairfield Council area in **August**. In a single morning, you could travel between China, Cambodia and Vietnam, savouring the unique character of each. Continue the sensuous feast at any of the local shopping areas, where the stench of durian fruit mixes with the salty smell of fresh fish and the pungent aroma of Asian barbecue. Many Australian natives favour the winter months, with boronias, wattles and eucalypts releasing their heady scents into the crisp winter air. Rug up and get out there.

As spring infuses **September**, it's time to celebrate with a trip to the Blue Mountains (see page 172), where many of the lovely old established gardens, particularly in Leura and Mt Wilson, are open for display. Carpets of freesias and bluebells fill the air with their delicate scent, mixing with the comforting smell from woodburning fireplaces. In the suburbs, the grass has started growing lush again, so Sunday morning spells the contrast between the annoying buzz of the mower

Eau du Ocean

We always thought the ocean got its invigorating smell from ozone, but learnt recently it's the far less-romantic-sounding dimethyl sulphide, which is released by (believe it or not) plankton when they're being attacked by larger sea creatures.

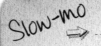

Slow-mo ⟹

Common Scents

- Stop and smell all the flowers, crush herbs and even leaves in your hand and breathe in the scent. You might not always smell anything, but when you do it'll put a spring in your step.

- Put your nose right up close to a flower or tree and fill your head with its scent. Grow your favourite flower and design your garden to be an aromatic wonderland.

- Go to one of the sourdough bakeries around town and just breathe.

- Lie on your back in the park, close your eyes and concentrate on the scents around you.

- Create a sanctuary in your home by burning your favourite oils and aromatic candles. Sprinkle a few drops of citrus oil on the floor of the shower, out of the water, and let the steam bring it alive to create a sensual, stimulating shower (albeit short). Make your own air freshener by mixing a few drops of a relaxing essential oil – like lavender or chamomile – with water in a spray bottle.

and the refreshing smell of newly mown grass. Add in the heady scent of jasmine, and we know summer is on the way.

The longer evenings of **October** and the arrival of spring blooms prompt late-afternoon strolls. Back in the RBG the ibises (the asylum seekers of the native bird world, having migrated east after losing much of their natural inland waterway habitation) pong but they look fantastic.

The smell of wet earth and clean air after a downpour in **November** creates millions of different perfumes, as every park, garden and backyard emits its own special fragrance. At this time of year – when most trees and flowers are in bloom – the stillness following a shower frames a spectacular, floral sweetness.

There's a real mix of aromas in **December**. As the holiday season starts to rev up, we begin to wind down – it's time to bring out the thongs and talcumy sunscreen, fire up the barbecue and throw on the snags. Some of

our less-appealing wildlife appears – hence the haze of citronella and mosquito coils in the air.

Three-quarters of Sydney visits the Fish Markets on Christmas Eve, where the air smells of the sea and the counters are stacked with dozens of varieties of sea creatures, as colourful and exotic as any tropical birds.

The other quarter steadfastly refuses to shift from tradition, and so we catch the odd whiff of old English food – there's nothing more confounding than the incongruous smell of Christmas pudding on a stinking hot Sydney day.

The quintessentially summer smells become more intense as we head towards December 31, and find ourselves in even more serious no-work mode. And as that clock ticks towards midnight, the skies of the city are filled with the sharp and unmistakably nostalgic tang of gunpowder, and the air is filled with optimism for a Happy New Year. ■

That Flower Stall

One of the busiest corners in Sydney also happens to be one of the sweetest-smelling. Depending on what time of the year you happen to be at the George St end of Martin Place, you'll get a gentle drift of hyacinth, lilies or roses in the air. They've been selling flowers here for who knows how long. The current stallholder, who'd rather not give his name but is well known to city workers, has been here "longer than you've been on the planet – 60 years, just after the war, I was nine years old when I started."

He used to help his father look after the stand, which in those days was a little wooden hut. At first it was a way of getting out of the house, he says, never imagining he'd still be here more than half a century later. When he first got involved, rent for the stall was ninepence a week – it's considerably more these days, for a permanent and more comfortable structure (with far less character than the old one). There's space for a table to cut and arrange the flowers, rails for the colourful ribbons and papers, a board to pin up family photos and an area outside for the big buckets of flowers.

There's been a lot of change in the area, too, not least the transformation of Martin Place into a pedestrian area in the 1970s. He has to keep up with the changes around him as much as floral fashion (gerberas aren't going so well these days) because inevitably the kiosk acts as an information booth. But don't even think of asking for a bargain on a bouquet at the end of the day. His reply will likely be, "With overtime, that'll be…"

Childhood memories for many Sydney-siders are filled with smells. Most have disappeared into the ether, often at the end of a developer's wrecking ball or via a brigade of designers who transformed the original olfactory factories into sanitised living spaces. Those memories include the smell of hops and yeast at the old Carlton Brewery on Broadway, of Wagon Wheels from the Weston Biscuit Factory in Camperdown, of mustards and relishes from Masterfoods in Matraville, and soap flakes from the Colgate Palmolive factory in Balmain.

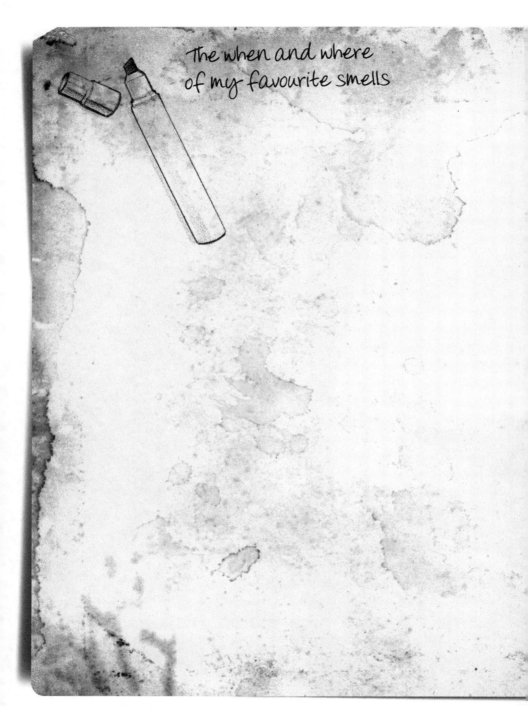

The when and where
of my favourite smells

TASTE
Characteristic Flavours

---•---

" GIVE ME SPOTS ON THE APPLES
BUT LEAVE ME THE BIRDS AND BEES. "

Joni Mitchell

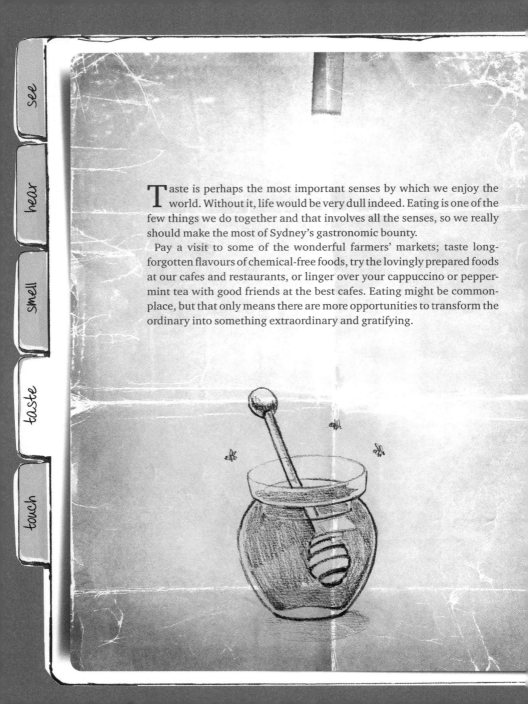

see

hear

smell

taste

touch

T aste is perhaps the most important senses by which we enjoy the world. Without it, life would be very dull indeed. Eating is one of the few things we do together and that involves all the senses, so we really should make the most of Sydney's gastronomic bounty.

Pay a visit to some of the wonderful farmers' markets; taste long-forgotten flavours of chemical-free foods, try the lovingly prepared foods at our cafes and restaurants, or linger over your cappuccino or peppermint tea with good friends at the best cafes. Eating might be common-place, but that only means there are more opportunities to transform the ordinary into something extraordinary and gratifying.

Slow Food Sydney

Sydney is gradually embracing the concepts popularised by Slow Food, the international movement that sprouted in Italy in 1986. When a McDonald's was slated to open beside Rome's beloved Spanish Steps, Italian food writer Carlo Petrini (no doubt yelling, crying, beseeching La Madonna and waving his arms around a lot) decided the culture of fast food had encroached too far.

The mass production, uniformity and blandness of international chains and supermarkets were too much for this passionate Italian to bear, and, brandishing bowls of penne, he led a protest urging consumers to consider the cost of 'convenience' and re-engage with their food.

Petrini's movement has grown roots around the globe, inspiring people to fight the industrialisation of the food chain, to connect with the local community, and to preserve flavour and diversity on the plate. Slow Food encourages people to be more mindful of what they do for nourishment, and to make time for communal meals and conviviality.

Slow food isn't a fashion statement: it is handcut sausages cooked over red-gum coals and served with local beer at a community fundraiser, says food writer Matthew Evans, an early proponent of slow food in Sydney, who describes his favourite slow Sydney restaurants on page 107. It's an expression of desire for community, culture and tradition – all the ingredients that used to be part of the ritual of eating. "It's getting a coffee and sitting down to drink it while you talk to the person who made it, rather than grabbing one on the run," says Evans. "It's taking time for you and them."

"Slow food is anything that's not fast food," according to Laurence McCoy, who is convivium leader of Slow Food Sydney, which holds dinners, talks and other events that promote the benefits of taking one's time over what we do for sustenance.

But, of course, you don't have to belong to any organisation to get the most out of your tastebuds – you can practise 'slow' whenever you're buying, preparing, enjoying or even thinking about food.

For his part, McCoy believes that "reducing food to fuel is like reducing love to sex". Slow food (or, may we say, good food) that is jam-packed with taste, "is concerned with bio-diversity and tradition; it is about experiencing food from different cultures; it is about the small-scale farmer," he says.

So, if you, too, believe in the ability of food to delight us with its flavours, to join us with friends and to unite community, rejoice in quality. Buy local and buy small, organise your own tastings of small-farm produce or wines, bring consciousness to your purchasing and eating habits, and respect food's importance in our lives.

Eating In

We all have to shop at a supermarket occasionally, but buying from specialists who are passionate about what they peddle is infinitely more rewarding, and brings a bit of magic to the everyday.

Markets

Supermarket chains suck. They suck the life out of agriculture, the community feeling out of shopping and, too often, the flavour out of food. Of course, there are some good local supermarkets but, in general, they don't support diversity and sustainability unless, of course, there's a good buck in it.

Whenever possible, purchase your food at a farmers' market that supports local growers and offers tasty, seasonal, local produce, some of it organic. Farmers' markets also present an opportunity to meet the people who produce the goods; there's nothing like having a chat to the producer of whatever it is you're going to eat or drink, whether it be a plum, an organic chicken, a bottle of wine or a cup of coffee.

Farmers' markets have the best slow credentials, but any option that shortens the supply chain and gives the consumer more choice is good in our book.

Warwick Farm Market *(Warwick Farm Racecourse, Governor Macquarie Drive; 8am-noon Sat)* is smaller than most, and utterly unpretentious. Expect biodynamic apples and cartons of plump figs, bite-sized apples "for lunchboxes", and local milk and cream. A stall sells celery, spring onions, corn and cabbage fresh from a farm at Camden; the Cowra Smokehouse has come with plump smoked trout. There's ham from Orange, salt-bush lamb, trays of free-range eggs and jars of family-made olive oil. Plus Turkish women making *gozleme* ('Turkish pancakes'), which attracts quite a crowd.

Although not organic, **Flemington Markets** (see page 94) has a plethora of fruit and vegies, and you can chat to the growers who tend them.

Manly West Organic Market *(Manly West Public School, Hill St, Balgowlah; 8am-1pm Sat)* is Australia's only fully certified and exclusively organic market. It's the place to buy organic ginger beer, La Tartine sourdough breads, Toby's Estate tea and coffee, and BeOrganic fruits and vegetables; there are plants, flowers and handmade jewellery for sale, too. After you've finished at the markets, Manly is a great spot for an ocean-side cappuccino.

Bondi Junction Organic Food & Farmers' Markets *(Oxford Street Mall, Bondi Junction; 9am-5pm Thurs-Sat)* sells organic and seasonal fruit and vegies, as well as meat, eggs and gourmet produce.

Leichhardt Farmers' Market *(Orange Grove Public School, Balmain Rd; 8am-1pm Sat)* is a thriving local market peddling organic foods including jams and chutneys, seasonal fruit and vegies, and teas and dried herbs. You can also pick up fresh flowers, recycled clothing and old wares.

Northside Produce Markets *(Civic Park, between Council Chambers and Stanton Library, Miller St, North Sydney; 8am-noon, third Sat)* offers locally produced cheeses, olives and oils, fresh and smoked seafood, fresh pasta and more from over 50 stallholders. You can grab a great cup of coffee, too, and there's usually plenty of nearby parking.

Cronulla Markets *(Cronulla High School, Bate Bay Rd; 9am-2pm, second and fourth Sun)* brings a taste of the country to the Sutherland shire with oodles of organic produce, poultry and meats, as well as value-added products like condiments, cakes and food from many nations (not to mention all sorts of crafts stalls and natural therapies).

You only need a whiff of that seafood smell at the famous **Sydney Fish Markets** *(cnr Pyrmont Bridge Rd and Bank Sts, Pyrmont; 7am-4pm daily)* to get you excited by the prospect of dinner. Around Christmas time, you can't get into the place as residents descend for bulk orders of fresh oysters, prawns and whole fish. And, be warned, the price of parking is prohibitive, so it's better to go by foot and combine your shopping trip with a little light exercise.

The fabulous **Good Living Growers Market** *(Pyrmont Foreshore, near Pyrmont Casino; 7-11am, first Sat)* really is worth inking in your diary every month (except January when they take a summer break). Up to a hundred stallholders offer award-winning meat, fish, fruit, vegetables, bread, cheese, jams and condiments, which taste all the more flavoursome when seasoned with the stories of the growers and producers.

City Night Markets *(Chinatown, Dixon St, Haymarket; 6-11pm Fri)* offer a vibrant mix of street theatre, fine food and outdoor dining.

Cabramatta

A visit to Cabramatta is like a round-the-world trip in your own city – more than 130 different nationalities call it home. In the lanes, alleyways and arcades around Hughes St and Railway Pde you'll be bombarded with the deliciously sharp smells of Chinese barbecue or chilli, and see everything from old men playing mah jong under a tree to Asian herbalists selling unidentifiable things from banks of drawers lining the walls of their shops. There's not much point listing favourites because you're unlikely to have a bad meal here. From salad with pork marinated in sesame seeds and lemongrass, to the avocado shake and the freshly cooked glutinous red-bean balls rolled in sesame seeds, there's something scrumptious and different to try every time. We always come away with a big bag of Asian delicacies, plus fresh fish, fruit and vegetables. Wander the streets around the main shops and you'll discover Buddhist temples in suburban houses, a lovely little community garden on Hughes St and a Russian Orthodox cathedral with gleaming gold onion domes.

Organics

Once upon a time organic food was considered to be a purely hippie or 'alternative' domain. But it is increasingly trading its sandals for a suit, with demand driven by food-safety scares, increasing awareness of its health benefits, a general discomfort with the genetically modified foods, environmental and animal-welfare issues, and overall a more mindful engagement with what we eat.

Organic consumers are no longer fringe-dwellers but everyone from business executives to gourmets. According to the Biological Farmers' Association, Australia's organic industry is currently valued at $300 million (although industry insiders say it's closer to $500 million), up from $28 million in 1995, and growing at between 15% and 25% each year.

That's big dollars, which is what we invariably think when we see the price tag on organics. But when it comes to what we put on our plate, it's quality not quantity that should define the experience.

What else would we purchase on price alone? We wouldn't buy the cheapest, crappiest mobile phone, so why apply that same stinginess to what we put in our bodies? Surely it's preferable to create meals from produce that has been grown or raised naturally, without artificial aids and toxic chemical and methods, and handled in a way that embodies respect for food.

Yes, it's more expensive to buy organic, and very few of us can afford to it all the time. But individually and collectively, we need to think more about what is best for our health, our community and our environment, and ask ourselves, can we afford *not* to introduce at least some organic produce in our diet?

Everything is so beautifully presented in the **Earth Food Store** *(81a Gould St, Bondi; 9130 2080)*, from the fresh herbs on the counter to the rows of organic fruit and vegetables displayed on the shelves, that just shopping here feels like a life-enhancing experience. Caroline Attwooll, a former theatre company director, opened the shop in 1991, and she brings some flair to this enterprise.

The only difference between this and a dramatic play is that it's the crisp, delicious produce that puts on a show and will no doubt have you calling for an encore. Bring your own cloth bags, and don't forget to visit Natural Progression next door (see page 133) for beauty and health products.

As you'd expect on the northern beaches, **Avalon Organics** *(25 Avalon Pde; 9918 3387)* has a wide selection of expensive organic produce, such as stone fruits, berries and zucchini flowers. Owner Michael Tansley-Witt is something of a pioneer in the industry, having opened this shop 10 years ago. He put another feather in his cap with the recent addition of an organic butchery.

The shop labels certified organic produce with a green sticker, and other produce, where the growers are converting to organic, with a red one. This increases the amount of chemical-free produce to customers and encourages farmers who are trying to shun toxic mass production.

"We are very much a gourmet food store, but one with our hearts in organic produce," says Michael. "Our produce is mostly picked the day before, we have a high turnover ensuring freshness and we are very discerning about what we buy." The sweet tomatoes, flavoursome cherries and crunchy apples all attest to Michael's keen ethic and eye.

Mooching Around the Market

We arrive at Flemington Markets at 7am, when Paul Carrano at Scala Bros has already served hundreds of rich, strong macchiatos. He's chatty, charming and anticipates what we want before we know – a lifesaver this early. It's wholesale day (retail days are Friday to Sunday) and some of the growers have been setting up their stalls since 1am.

Paul took over the business from his dad, Andrea, now 80, who has fed the hordes of wholesalers, growers and buyers since 1956. Andrea is still around: "We make him count the money," Paul laughs. We sit at the outdoor tables, eating toasted Italian bread topped with tomato and cheese and sprinkled with oregano and a drizzle of olive oil, while Paul brings more strong coffee.

We sit alongside older men who look like extras from a Fellini movie. Inside, people are picking up everything from Scorpion Mezcal to pasta, oils, nuts, cheeses and homemade woodfired bread – much of it in bulk. You can get panettone and Quovadis Sambucca, plus mini gelato cones in Sicilian chocolate.

Scala Bros is set to the side of the markets – enormous warehouses with concrete flooring and big cardboard boxes of produce whizzed around by kamikaze-style forklift drivers. Weekends are the big days for the public, who come for competitively priced fruit, vegetables and flowers and the experience of shopping in a noisy, colourful market.

The flowers have their own hall, not far from Scala Bros, and you can almost drink in the perfume emanating from the petals of roses, orchids, gerberas and carnations; brilliant reds and oranges, sunny yellows and lavender blues.

The cavernous, sprawling fruit and vegie pavilions echo the hustle, bustle and exuberance. Among the goods, you can get at least a dozen varieties of mushrooms (from shiitake and enoki to Swiss browns), half a dozen varieties of potatoes, and dozens of different herbs, all first-hand from growers.

Brothers George and David Macri sell chestnuts and olives, as well as fresh fruit and veg; their father gave them each a stall at opposite ends of the market so they wouldn't bicker while they worked. Nearby, Marie does a roaring trade in zucchini flowers, which she's only to happy to show off. A garrulous herb grower from Windsor sells tarragon, chervil and sage or whatever he deems "the next big thing". He's kind of like a fashion forecaster for herbs. "Rocket and basil – that's over," he decrees. "Everyone's doing that now. We've moved on."

Then there's the huge Moraitis business, run mostly by fast-talking Italians – they have their own coffee machine and masses of fresh produce brimming from boxes.

Flemington Markets (*1300 361 589*) are near Homebush Bay, 15km west of the CBD. Follow the signs to Sydney Markets from Parramatta Rd, the M4 motorway or Centenary Drive. Or catch a train to Flemington City Rail Station next to the Sydney Markets.

'Real' bread is the epitome of slow. Its critical ingredient (yeast starter) is a living organism that can bubble away for years and which gives the bread its fickle but usually fabulous nature (it rises when *it's* ready). Real bread has a character of its own, with every loaf looking slightly different, and with a texture to get your teeth into. Walk into one of Sydney's bona fide bakeries, breathe in the aroma of freshly baked bread, and just try to walk out empty-handed.

At **Brasserie Bread Co** (*1737 Botany Rd, Banksmeadow; 9666 6845*), the sourdough baker's round was the 2006 Champion Loaf at the Sydney Royal Bread, Cake & Pie Competition (somebody tell us how you get to be a judge for that!) and the bakery got the guernsey for the most successful bread exhibitor at the same show. Anything Brasserie makes is delicious, and its cafe is one of our favourite places to eat, with the winning combination of the best toast around, outstanding coffee and the opportunity to watch the bakers work their magic.

As soon as you taste the soy-and-linseed bread, with its whole soybeans (non-GM, of course), at **Sonoma Baking Company** (*215a Glebe Point Rd, Glebe; 9660 2116 and 24/198 Young St, Waterloo; 9690 2060*) you'll be hooked. The bonus is, you'll feel healthier for eating it. The spelt loaf's a good one, too – nice and chewy and nutty. Spelt is probably the oldest grain in the world, having first been grown about 5000 BC. Sonoma's spelt loaves take three days to make – nothing this good happens overnight. There are good cafes at both outlets, too.

For a complete change of loaf, **Sapori di Pane** (*Shop 5, 44-46 the Horsley Drive, Carramar; 9728 4858*) specialises in old-fashioned southern Italian bread. The recipes come mainly from postwar migrants, who've kept everything exactly as it was when they left the 'old country'. The rustic loaf, with its serious crust that gives your gums a serious workout, is particularly good. Sapori also serves pizza slices, cannoli, various biscotti and all sorts of other tasty treats. And while you're here, it's well worth stocking up at the *pastizzi* (savoury-filled pastry) place next door.

All sorts of sourdough loaves (including walnut), plus excellent cakes, individual pizzas and baguettes (that actually have a bit of substance to them), can be found at **Infinity Sour Dough Bakery** (*225 Darlinghurst Rd, Darlinghurst; 9380 4320*). And in that part of the city that never sleeps, it's a great relief to find Infinity open – you'd hate to run out of the stuff.

Slow Affirmations

Eat every meal like it's your first.
Order by name, not by number.
Respect the rhythm of the seasons when buying ingredients.

Mass-produced meat is the antithesis of slow, which is where butchers like Mc-Donagh's Meat Boutique *(119b North Rd, Ryde; 9878 3533)* come in. Manager Shane Younger buys slow-bred pork from a family-run business in the Riverina and lamb from specially selected farms in Cowra. The shop only stocks free-range, hormone- and antibiotic-free chicken from the Lilydale brand, and its sausages are all gluten-free and made with high-quality meat. It's owned by an Irish family, so you'll also find some Dublin cheeses and award-winning black and white puddings.

Butcher Sam Diasinos of **Sam the Butcher** *(San Souci, Bondi, Beecroft and Naremburn; www.samthebutcher.com.au; 9583 1144)* is from a long line of meat retailers, and follows proudly in the steps of his father and grandfather before him.

But what distinguishes Sam is that he was one of the first Sydney butchers to sell organic meat, opening his Sans Souci store in 1991. Nothing is prepackaged and there's an extensive selection for conscious carnivores: from duck and gourmet sausages to prime beef and lamb. Sam also uses family recipes to make things like chicken-liver pâté and Umbrian lamb shanks.

Send in the Cones

What would a sticky, summer day in Sydney be without ice cream? Not just any old ice cream but mint chocolate chip, cassata, Belgian chocolate, coconut or pistachio from Salvatore and Ciccio at Gelatomassi *(262 King St, Newtown; 9516 0655)*. Ciccio always has a line for the ladies, while the male clientele amuse themselves mulling over flavours in the two long cases of cool, creamy treats. It's all made fresh on the premises and the fruit flavours are all seasonal. Ciccio's favourite: honey-roasted almond. Customers' favourite: the Sundae Siciliana of hazelnut, pistachio, cassata and roasted almond gelato with chocolate shavings. Ciccio and Sal are the grandsons of Salvatore Las Rosa, who came to Australia from Sicily in the 1950s as a carpenter and ended up opening La Rustica restaurant in Leichhardt. They previously worked at another Sydney favourite, Rossinis by the Quay.

Great whirling mounds of gelato compete for attention alongside giant cakes of fruit and marzipan, cannoli and Italian shortbread at the Pasticceria Papa *(145 Ramsay St, Haberfield; 9798 6894)*. Try vanilla, lemon, tiramisu or pistachio, and revel in the continuous flow of Italian bonhomie. Opened in 1994 by Siciliana Salvatore Papa this patisserie appeals not only to the Italian community but also to sweet-toothed locals.

Head to Patagonia Ice Cream & Cafe *(231 Coogee Bay Rd, Coogee; 9665 5797)* for locally made pistachio, mascarpone and fig, and a *dulce de leche* – thick caramel – that will give you a sugar high for the rest of the afternoon.

Delis

From Glacé ice cream and gourmet pâtés to Yulla tahini and corn-fed chicken, the **Barn Cafe & Grocery** *(731-735 Darling St, Rozelle; www.thebarncafe.com.au; 9810 1633)* has a little bit of every "good, wholesome food" you can think of, says co-owner and chef Brenda Millett. "We set up the Barn to give locals a place to call their own, where they could sit, read the newspaper and have a coffee, but also know that it is a place where things happen." Some of the profits are returned to the community through sponsorship or community events. There are also cooking classes for kids, singles and "committed couples" that are usually booked up well in advance.

Vibrant red walls and Gauguin-style paintings, *courvature* (hot chocolate) served with freshly prepared *churros*, plus every Spanish cheese available in Australia, all make **Delicado Foods** *(Shop 2/134 Blues Point Rd, McMahons Point; 9955 9399; www.delicadofoods.com.au)* the pre-eminent Spanish deli. It is run by the President of the Australian Sommeliers Association, Ben Moechtar, and his partner Ambie Moore and, since opening in 2005, has developed quite a cult following. There are fresh and cured meats from Rodriguez Brothers, slow-produced Jamon Iberico and organic breads from La Tartine; a tiny cafe, crowded with art and thick with European atmosphere; tapas and wine-tasting workshops; Spanish classes; and plans for a boutique bottle shop. You can even get a picnic hamper to take away, maybe to the nearby Secret Garden (see page 123).

Cheese-lovers should go straight to the back of Rozelle's **Fine Foods** *(4/595 Darling St; 9810 2858)*. In the 15°C storeroom, food technologist and local Kerri Clark is happy to guide buyers through a taste tour of some of the best cheeses that money can buy in Sydney. In store there's also baba ganoush, flavoured olive oils, the best balsamic vinegars and a range of cookbooks.

Something Special

Anna-maria Eoclidi's family hails from Emilia-Romagna, and she uses the family's recipes to make tortellini, ravioli and lasagne, as well as deliciously rustic pasta sauces, at **Pasta Emilia** *(129 Macpherson St, Bronte; 0415 286 268)*.

A must for fans of small delicacies, such as Portuguese custard tarts, **Sweet Belem** *(35 New Canterbury Rd, Petersham; 9572 6685)* is named after the Lisbon suburb where the owners used to live, and is decorated with Portuguese-style tiling and pictures. Their pastries are made on the premises, and you have the option of washing them down with a bottle of Portuguese semi-sparking white.

Cross the threshold into **Herbies Spices** *(745 Darling St, Rozelle; 9555 6035)* and you will feel like you're being bathed in exotic pot pourri. It's thanks to the olfactory notes of more than 235 spices jammed onto the shelves. According to Jacqui Newling, who takes spice appreciation classes here (see page 140): "Lots of shops are dedicated to certain cuisines, but we try to have it all." There's a whole row of chilli spices alone; on others cardamom, bay leaves, saffron, vanilla bean, rose petals, tamarind, dried porcini mushrooms and a seductively sweet and sour *amchur* powder (dried green mango) jostle for attention. Herbies is owned by author Ian Hemphill, whose parents have been in the herb and spice scene since the 1950s.

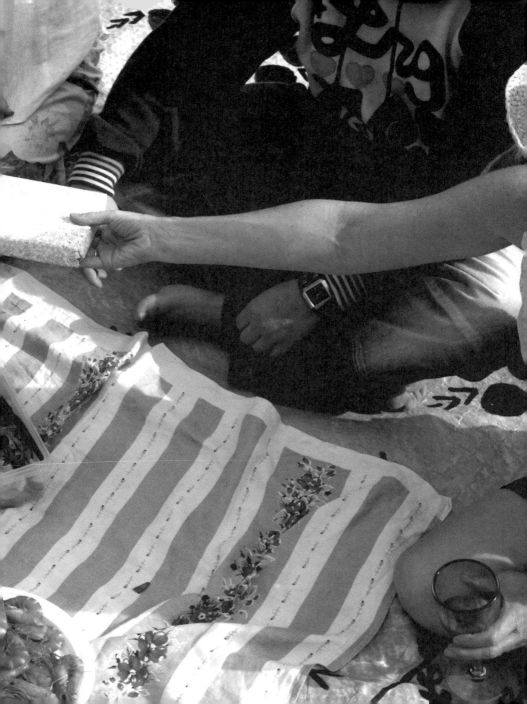

Essay →

It's a Famiglia Affair

The wine press resembles an item from a collector's catalogue, its oak panels beautifully burnished by decades of red grapes being pummelled through its barrel. Seventy-five-year-old Saverio Cipri (pictured) has been using it for 40 years, at his home in Croydon Park, to make his shiraz/merlot. Today it is standing in the middle of the family garage, brimming with ripe, purple fruit, as his son, chef Carmelo, 35, and son-in-law, panelbeater Frank Ianelli, 48, get down to the serious business of making wine.

First, a glass or two of canary-yellow limoncello (lemon liqueur) to warm the blood. Then the press is applied to the top of the ruddy pile and a rich, jewel-coloured juice drips out the bottom of the contraption and into large plastic tubs. The bucketed juice will be cleaned of sludge about

three or four times in the next two weeks before it is poured into stainless-steel barrels to continue fermenting for up to four months. The resulting alcoholic nectar, which is sugar- and preservative-free, is about 18% proof, Carmelo tells us, and is served out of unlabelled bottles to a family of close-knit Calabrians. "We may make labels for it eventually," says Carmelo. "But, right now…" Well, right now they're happy just to drink it.

Nearby are Saverio and his wife Maria, 62, who have been in Australia for 45 years. "We got married when I was 16, seven weeks after we met in our hometown of Palmi," smiles Maria. "This country is home to me now but I still like to make the traditional food for our family."

She and youngest son Anthony, 33, who is front-of-house at Swordfish El Ristorante

(see page 106), the Kingsford restaurant that he owns with Carmelo, are quartering ripe tomatoes and feeding them through a *spremipomodoro passatutto* (tomato press). The end product will be a pasta sauce so thick and tangy that little addition is needed besides a bit of home-grown basil and salt. Before then, there is elbow grease to be applied, the kind that goes into creating traditional home-made ingredients. Saverio tells us: "I go to a restaurant and I don't like the sauce they have on the pasta. It is too full of chemicals. It is not good." Carmelo nods in agreement.

Near the work table is a charcoal grill with giant stainless-steel pots on top. Explains Maria: "The tomatoes are partly cooked, then we put them through the press three or four times to get every bit of their juice and pulp." By some kind of mechanical miracle, the tomato skins are spat out the back of the machine and only the flesh of the tomato makes it into the bowl Maria has placed beneath the press. "We should get an electric press, Mama," says Anthony, who has the job of turning the handle on the press over and over again. "No, no," says Maria. "The hand one, it is better. I like the traditional ways." Anthony shrugs. "When we used to help with this as children, we had a day off from school."

He breaks from his labour to offer us a taste of last year's chilli pesto, made from parsley and gigantic, crushed basil leaves that grow in the Cipris' compact backyard. The pesto is so hot our mouths burn and our eyes tear up. "That is the mild one,"

laughs Maria. Saverio grows the chillies for this fierce mix, along with the fennel, mint, rosemary and bay, and, each year, collects seeds from the herbs to plant once more.

The bubbling tomato pulp is ready. Maria and Anthony pour it into sterilized bottles that they then place in another big stainless-steel tub, cover with water and a tea towel, and then set to boil for an hour. The bottles will last for up to a year.

The couple has another son, Joe, 43, and two daughters, Carmel, 41, and Mimma, 44. Add in the grandchildren, says Maria, and "there's usually about 18 of us at the dinner table. Feeding that many, it's a lot of work! But I always work hard, even when I was a girl."

"Here, try these," offers Carmelo, who is holding a plate of fat green olives. Yes, the family makes them. "Put the olives in water for a couple of days to clean out the chemicals," instructs Maria. "Then change the water, and add enough sea salt so that a fresh egg floats to the top." Add a piece of chilli and garlic and two months later, you have marinated olives. "They will keep all year because of the salt."

In a morning's work, there's wine, rows of pasta sauce and tubs of olives waiting to be enjoyed around a family table that buzzes with love and Italiano.
HELEN HAWKES

Carmelo buys ingredients for the family at Flemington Markets (see page 94). You can buy equipment to make your own wine at Merilux *(15 Parramatta Rd, Haberfield; 9712 2333)*.

Eating Out

What defines an eating establishment as 'slow' is subjective, so, here are some of our favourite, traditional and relaxing places to enjoy good grub seasoned with a little local character.

Relaxed

Cook & Archies *(Shop 1a, 4 Buckingham St, Surry Hills; 9310 3933)* makes simply delicious homemade lunches, with daily specials that include at least three yummy, wholesome salads (like mixed greens, cherry tomatoes, avocado, beetroot and haloumi served with fresh sourdough bread) and usually a lasagne or pasta bake. The décor is basic, but there are lots of windows with light pouring in, and the fact that it has a communal table and is a little off the beaten track makes it even more appealing.

The **Bald Rock Hotel** *(17 Mansfield St, Rozelle; 9818 4792)* is daggy. Wonderfully so. With its sandstone walls, homely fire and roast of the day with a glass of wine for around $15, it's not out to compete with the look-at-me atmosphere of other trendier pubs. Don your most comfortable pair of jeans and favourite T-shirt, and head over for a Sunday evening at the hotel with a few good friends to tell stories and have a decent feed. The front bar is small and dimly lit, the bar staff are friendly and you can eat in the beer garden or in the little room with the fire. Don't miss the photographs of other old pubs that have stood the test of time, as well as those which have, sadly, given way to the kind of places where it's considered okay to drink beer with a piece of lime.

Natural

At **Peasant's Feast** *(121a King St; 9516 5998)* in Newtown, the décor evokes the feeling of a farmhouse feel and the food is pesticide- and chemical-free. Even the water used for the cooking is double filtered. Owner Dr Robert Warlow, a clinical immunologist, allergist and medical researcher, believes this is the only "medicalised" restaurant in Australia. "Organic ingredients are only part of it," he says. "The way we cook the food – slowly, with no sugar and nothing deep fried – is also important." Try the delicious spinach parcel, raw salads, mushroom pie, vegetarian platter or organic meat dishes. They also cater for special diets and takeaways.

Iku Wholefoods *(Glebe, Neutral Bay, Darlinghurst, Rozelle, Waverley and the CBD)* uses hundreds of organic, biodynamic and natural ingredients, and matches ethics with the slow food ideal. Try the casserole of chickpea, coriander and sweet potato, or the Macro Burger of tofu fritter, green salad and tahini on steamed organic spelt.

After laps in the Cook & Phillip Park pool, sustain the healthy feeling at **Bodhi's Restaurant and Bar** *(College St; 9360 2523)*, a vegan yum cha eatery next door, serving fresh rice-noodle folds and steamed peanut buns. Buddha heads mingle with muted shades indoors, or you can eat under umbrellas outdoors.

Charmers

From the wonderfully kitsch china doves in the window to the salami and tomato panini, refrigerated cakes groaning with glacé fruit and elaborately wrapped chocolates, a visit to **A&P Sulfaro Pasticceria Italiana** *(119 Ramsay St, Haberfield; 9797 0001)* is a little piece of Italy. Join the Italian mamas at the outdoor tables eating great mounds of tiramisu from brightly coloured plastic cups and you'll feel like you are living *la dolce vita*. Order a coffee, ask for the panini toasted and watch the old Italian men over the road at the *cremeria* (tea and coffee place) while they watch you. This family business was started in 1971 by owner Antonio Sulfaro and is still going strong.

Sicilian mother-and-son team, Maria and Carmelo Cipri, draw from family history at **Swordfish El Ristorante** *(Level 2, 558 Anzac Pde, Kingsford; 9344 4404)*. Carmelo tried other kitchen staff but realised Mama always knows best when it comes to the grill. There's plenty to love, like a grilled snapper with brown mushrooms and snow peas. The tiramisu, flourless chocolate cake and other desserts are homemade. (See It's a Famiglia Affair on page 102 for more on the family.)

You'll need time to eat your way through the Sultan's Banquet at one of Parramatta's best ethnic restaurants, **Sahra** *(Shop 2, 76 Phillip St; 9635 6615)*, which specialises in Middle Eastern cuisine. Friendly owner Talal Alamein will guide you through 12 traditional hot and cold dishes, including chicken done in pomegranate, walnut sauce and saffron. Weekends are best, when you can mix wonderful ethnic food with a little of the esoteric – there's a fortune teller and a bellydancer.

Bill & Toni's *(74 Stanley St, East Sydney; 9360 4702)* feels like a little working men's cafe in Italy – there are no frills, just really good, basic, genuine Italian food. You might fish the odd bayleaf out of the bolognese, as this lovely, aromatic stuff definitely doesn't come out of a jar. Decades old, Bill & Toni's attracts an unlikely mix from skateboarders to barristers and happy families.

Palisade Hotel *(35 Bettington St, Millers Point; 9247 2272)* is stuck out like a shag on a rock, so it's managed to escape all the commercialisation of the Rocks. The slightly austere interior feels exactly like an Australian pub should. You'll always find a few locals sitting around chewing the fat and being disdainful of the type of blow-ins who see the area as a real estate haven.

Original

There aren't many ritzier holiday places in Sydney than Palm Beach, or Balmie Palmie as the locals and the holidaymakers (the Packers, the Kidman/Urbans et al.) like to think of it.

Which is partly why the burgers like-mum-used-to-make-'em at the **General Store** *(1118 Barrenjoey Rd, Palm Beach; 9974 1016)* come as such a pleasant surprise. It's not gnocchi with truffle oil; it's grilled meat with tomato, onion, beetroot, bacon, egg and barbecue sauce all packed into a bun.

Yeasty, firm and often chewy, a freshly made bagel is a beautiful way to start the day, or even end it. Some of the best bagels in Sydney can be found at **Mendel Glick's** *(173 Bondi Rd, Bondi; 9386 9949)*. If you're passing between 9pm and midnight on a Saturday and need a snack to help you on your way, call in for fresh bagels and pizza.

A Friend Recommends...

There can be no definitive list of best slow restaurants in Sydney because, while bound up in a more mindful approach to eating, there are different interpretations of slow. Matthew Evans, former restaurant critic and chef who is currently making his living as a freelance food and travel writer for various publications, was one of the first proponents of slow food in Sydney. Here are his five slow Sydney highlights.

SEAN'S PANAROMA *(270 Campbell Pde, Bondi Beach; 9365 4924)*

Sean Moran is a professional cook who embodies the attitude of home cooking with none of its inherent risk. In his cute, beach-chic space with Bondi Beach views, the focus is on flavour, flavour, produce and flavour. Every dish is complete, no extra vegetables, no going home hungry, no wondering what the meat should taste like.

BILLY KWONG *(Shop 3, 355 Crown St Surry Hills; 9332 3300)*

Kylie Kwong's Asian bistro is founded on slow principles – hospitality, egalitarianism and organic or biodynamic produce when available. Like a dark, modern teahouse, using her home-style Chinese cooking and the ingredients as inspiration, it's a heady ride. That you can't book and have to sit on button stools, just adds to its allure.

DANKS STREET DEPOT *(1/2 Danks St, Waterloo; 9698 2201)*

Jared Ingersoll's proudly produce-focused menu is like no other. He attempts to harness the best of an ingredient, be it a broad bean or a hunk of Speck, using age-old techniques with no hint of fake flavours or shortcuts. That it comes at cafe prices would be embarrassing if it wasn't for the fact that you're the one paying.

CAFÉ SOPRA *(7 Danks St, Waterloo; 9699 3174)*

Above the food importer and greengrocer Fratelli Fresh, Sopra's emphasis is on Italian-style food, packed with flavour and the freshness you'd expect from one of Sydney's finest food emporiums. Check out what chef Andy Bunn can do with the ingredients and try to recreate it at home.

WHARF PIER *(4 Hickson Rd, Walsh Bay; 9250 1761)*

Despite its glossy harbourside location and Harbour Bridge views, Tim Pak Poy's waterfront restaurant isn't short on cred. Home of the annual NSW truffle dinner, Pak Poy showcases rare-breed pork, the finest techniques and an uncommon sense of what food means to both consumers and growers. Deft and sometimes confronting, it's as individual as his time at Claude's, without the culinary tightwire act.

Matthew Evans has two books out with Random House in late 2007: *Never Order Chicken on a Monday*, an insight into his life in and out of kitchens; and *The Weekend Cook*, a collection of recipes from his much loved column in *Good Weekend*.

Cafes

Thirty-odd years ago, you could buy decent hamburgers in every Sydney suburb. But then McDonald's arrived, and everyone forgot what a real hamburger was meant to taste like.

If we're not careful, the same thing could happen with coffee, as the big chains come in and serve up dozens of different styles and flavours of coffee in more sizes than we need. We'd much rather spend our time in the local, one-off alternative – cafes with personality, individuality and the best coffee around (none of that flavoured rubbish) served at just the right temperature in a normal-sized cup or glass. And we don't even mind a bit of attitude occasionally – at least it's human and real.

We might be into slow, but that doesn't extend to queues, so when Walter moved to a much bigger place up the road, we were thrilled. The walnut toast with do-it-yourself avocado, hard-boiled egg, ricotta, tomato and tapenade sums up the fresh and simple approach of **Uliveto** *(33 Bayswater Rd, Potts Point; 9357 7331)*, although we have to say their cakes are utterly unforgettable. So, too, is everyone who works there – sometimes it feels as if you're surrounded by slightly eccentric but very loyal and lovable relatives.

As well as having good coffee, roasted onsite and available to take home, **Single Origin** *(60-64 Reservoir St, Surry Hills; 9211 0665)* even makes you feel good about drinking it – it's all Fair Trade, which is a big plus, and the milk is organic. Other bonuses are the Sonoma bread, used for all toast and sandwiches, and the completely delicious home-baked muesli.

At **Gertrude and Alice** *(40 Hall St, Bondi Beach; 9130 5155)* the biggest challenge is avoiding getting fingerprints on the books after an indulgent and calorific chocolate brownie. Grab a seat at a communal table or on the couch if you can, order some of the malty coffee, and settle in with some light reading from the bestsellers list or a more academic classic. The cafe is called Gertrude and Alice after early-20th-century lesbians Gertrude Stein and Alice Tolkas, and, besides appetising vegetarian food, features new, old and rare books.

The lovely, light-filled **Two Good Eggs** *(148 Goulburn Street, Surry Hills; 9283 9694)* is on the ground floor of a Philippe Starck-renovated apartment building, but it's not nearly as pretentious as that makes it sound. The kitchen is bigger than you might expect, so as well as turning out the best poached eggs in town, it also serves an imaginative, and regularly changing, lunchtime menu that never fails to impress and entice. And they use only the freshest of ingredients.

Just when you think you're done and stated, there's sure to be something equally-tempting on the counter to take away – last time it was impossible to resist the marzipan bunnies at Easter.

It's quite okay that **Wall** *(80 Campbell Street, Surry Hills; 9280 1980)* is a Melbourne import, because if there's one thing that city knows, it's what it takes to make a good cafe. Wall might be funky – that sunken conversation pit is a talking point in itself – but it's laid-back and friendly, rather than self-conscious or try-hard. Rely on great coffee, groovy artwork and deliciously savoury combinations in the pides. ∎

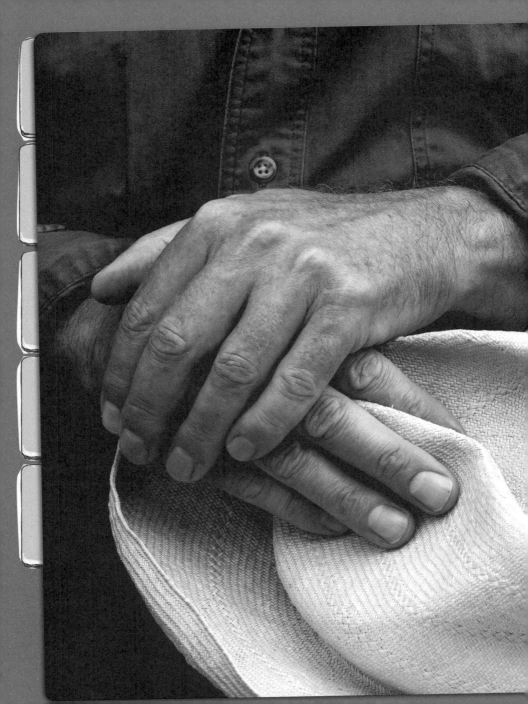

TOUCH
Feel Good

---·---

" **ONE TOUCH OF NATURE MAKES THE WHOLE WORLD KIN.** "

William Shakespeare

see

hear

smell

taste

touch

Touch can be a sign of friendship, affection, warmth or intimacy, but it can also be used therapeutically to help settle stress, according to Dr Craig Hassed, a senior lecturer at Monash University Medical Centre and international mind–body medicine expert. Touching and being touched can lift your mood, calm anxieties and strengthen your immune system. After all, what compares to the comfort of a hug or the vitality of a lover's touch?

In a city where people often rush past each other on any given day's urgent mission, fiercely protecting their personal space, the opportunity to touch and be touched can seem limited, Hassed says. And because many city dwellers now live alone, the chance for social or physical contact at home has also been reduced. Our increasingly virtual world further robs us of the chance to touch.

Yet, if we open ourselves up to it, everywhere in the city there are opportunities to be touched figuratively, to have our heartstrings plucked by beauty and the pathos of urban life. Let's also rediscover the tactile pleasures of living in Sydney: the opportunities to commune with nature, enjoying the sensation of the beach, feeling a sculpture designed to be touched, and even pressing flesh after a game of touch footy in the park.

Tactile

City

Perhaps the best place to start any touching tour of Sydney is in Pitt St with a hug from the world-famous **Juan Mann** (a play on words, pronounced 'one man') who offers free hugs to passers-by. His rules are: no names, no phone numbers, no relationships and no dates. His cuddling campaign has featured on YouTube and 'Good Morning America', reminding international audiences of the restorative qualities of human contact, even if only fleetingly.

To feel the embrace of nature, go to the nearest coast, remove your shoes and scrunch the sand through your toes. Bend deeply along the shoreline as you search for ridged, twirled, narrow and curvaceous shells, picking up each find and 'seeing' it with both hands. If the weather is balmy, throw your body into the cooling ocean and feel the salt water caress your skin and the stresses of the day wash away. Let yourself float in the ocean's arms, the water wrapping around you like a lover.

Take friends for a game of touch footy at the beach or a nearby park where you can enjoy the thwump of the ball against your palm, or the crash tackle of social footy (with obligatory handshakes and claps on the back afterwards).

If you're not afraid that others will think you are slightly touched yourself, hug a tree. "You can use your hands to discover not just the texture but the character of a tree," says Nicholas Gleeson of Vision Australia, who has been blind since aged seven. "Use your other senses, too – smell the gum on the bark, listen to the wind rustling through the leaves."

Travel up Oxford St to **Centennial Parklands** and you can wallow in 220 hectares of grass and plantations, including more than 10,000 trees. There are Moreton Bay and Port Jackson figs, paperbarks, flooded gums, pines, oaks and the splashily colourful coral trees.

The bark of a coral tree is smooth and grey although the older, taller trees can sometimes be like humans – a little prickly. So feel your

Touch Therapy

Massage is one of the oldest of the healing arts dating back to 3000 BC in Chinese history. Even Hippocrates, who was born in 460 BC and is widely known as the father of medicine, is believed to have endorsed the practice by stating that all physicians should have experience in 'rubbing' techniques. In Sydney, getting a massage treatment (see Salons and Spas, page 131) is one of the easiest ways to connect with another human being and get a boost of endorphins through the sense of touch.

way gently around the trunk. As you touch the 'coral', imagine the brilliant-red, pea-shaped flowers that form in clusters in spring, then the leaves, a green broad wedge shape, that follow once the petals have dropped.

You can also ride a horse at the Lang-Rd end of the park, with **Centennial Stables** (www .centennialstables.com.au; 9360 5650), one of the few parklands in the world to offer inner-city horse-riding. Sit astride a mare as you canter gently along the carriageways, stroking the animal's mane or patting its flank as you encourage it on an early morning spring or autumn ride. With fog in the hollows of the park and above the ponds you get a clear view, as if above the clouds, of treetops and the city skyline. The silence, save for the footfall of your mount and the creak of leather, add to the experience of solitude and space.

If you love dogs, head to any open area of the park and get licked and nuzzled and sometimes bowled over by the enthusiastic participants of catch and fetch. If you've got some affection to spare, volunteer at the **Sydney Dogs Home** (77 Edward St, Carlton; 9587 9611) any morning of the week and walk the homeless pooches.

For the kind of up-close-and-personal experience you don't usually get with furry and feathered birds and mammals, call into the **Australian Museum** (College St) and take the lift to the Search and Discover exhibition on the second floor. Unlike the displays in many museums, here you are actually encouraged to feel the soft fur of a fox, the rather stubby body of a koala and the magnificent, smooth plumage of a wedge-tailed eagle, all preserved for this extraordinary interactive gallery.

Beaches and Hidden Coves

Nowhere appeals to our sense of touch quite like the beach, and there's no better way of escaping into fantasies of childish adventures than exploring your own 'secret' cove.

Point the compass north towards Manly and the protected western shore of **North Head**. Paradoxically, today's escape is home to a Quarantine Station that was used for more than 150 years from 1828 to contain travellers deemed temporarily unfit to mingle with the general population. So there's kind of an eerie, historic feel to it. You can imagine the poor buggers holed up here for weeks and sometimes months, quarantined for influenza and other infectious disease. But at least they had a view.

Today, you can explore the station or get away from the crowd at the bay of Spring Cove. It was known to the original inhabitants as Kayoo-may and is named after the small waterfall onto the sand that is fed by a creek in the hills.

Much of the land here is covered by scrub, woodland and open forest that runs down to the rocky foreshores; you'll also see the last significant beds of sea grass in Sydney Harbour. You'll have to brush past the twigs and branches of native bush on a track to the eastern side of North Head to get to Spring Cove although you can also get here by **kayak** (www.sydneyharbourkayaks.com.au), which involves the delicious splash of salt water across your skin.

At the north end of the cove, you'll find Collins Beach and, in between Collins and Quarantine Beach, to the south, Store Beach. Get to the last by a rugged rock climb and, no doubt, a couple of scrapes on your knees

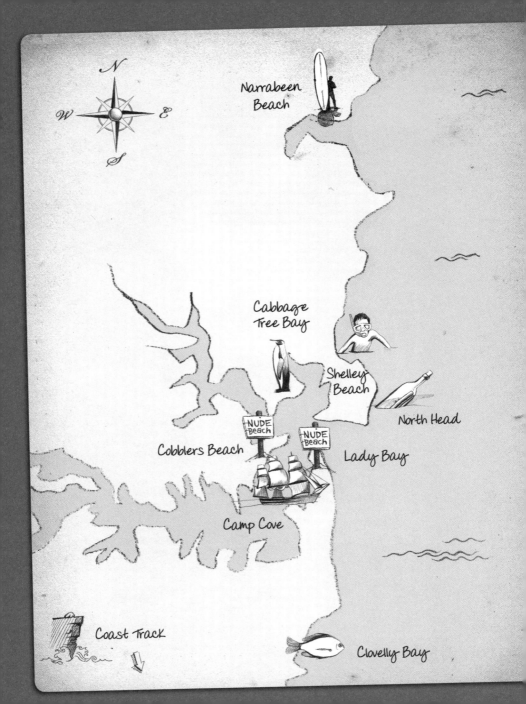

Narrabeen Beach

Cabbage Tree Bay

Shelley Beach

North Head

NUDE Beach

NUDE Beach

Cobblers Beach

Lady Bay

Camp Cove

Coast Track

Clovelly Bay

and elbows, from Collins Beach. Once you're there, sink your teeth into a home-made cheese-and-pickle sandwich and down some old-fashioned lemonade, while you dig your toes into the crunchy sand and enjoy the solitude. And be grateful you're not interred in the quarantine station!

On the east side of the city, at **Camp Cove** (*near Cliff and Victoria Sts in Watsons Bay*), you can also see the shoreline through the eyes of the early settlers. Captain Arthur Phillip and the First Fleet anchored here before landing at Sydney Cove in 1788. Before it was dominated by new immigrants, this area provided abundant fish, shellfish and food for the Aboriginal community. There's a rock shelter at the northern end of the beach that the Indigenous people once used; you may like to sit in it and ponder Australia of yesteryear, before whitefellas turned up.

In the south, the 30km **Coast Track** from Bundeena to Otford leads you to a gem of a cove and camping area. It runs the length of the Royal National Park's coastline, passing through Little Marley and Marley Beach, Wattamolla, Burning Palms and Garie, and the view is all native bush and smashing coastlines. The whole trek will take you about two days, but two hours in you can reach Little Marley and Marley Beach, pitch a tent, boil your billy and practise your whittling. You did bring the Swiss army knife didn't you?

Or take it easy on the sands of **Cronulla**, a stretch made famous in Kathy Lette's *Puberty Blues*. It and **Bondi Beach** are tops for studying Australian life, with displays as elaborate and competitive as any wildlife doco.

Narabeen Beach is name-checked by the Beach Boys and is one of the best places to feel the wax of a surf board beneath your feet

and the crush of waves against your body. Champions like Mark Warren, Damien Hardman and Simon Anderson have let the waves lick their toes here, and you, too, can feel the thundering caress of a tube on the shores of this northern beaches hangout.

For Jacques Cousteau–style marine adventure, head to family-friendly **Shelley Beach** in Manly. Australia's only west-facing beach on the east coast, it's filled with eastern blue groper, weedy sea dragon and gloomy octopus. You can snorkel or scuba dive and get a great view of the 'locals' because the water is so clear and shallow. You can also rent a kayak at Manly, an almost old-fashioned seaside resort that accepts all-comers. No 'tude – just sun, surf and a smoothie to chill you from inside out.

Pleasure seekers can take a 30-minute ride on the Manly Ferry to Circular Quay where both the view and the aroma of sea salt will thrill the senses; browse among the weekend craft market; or motor along the North Head Scenic Drive with its spectacular ocean and city views. We recommend an open-top car, with the wind whipping through your hair.

You can get even closer to nature at **Lady Bay** in the eastern suburbs, one of only three legal nude beaches in Sydney (good luck hiding the Swiss army knife). The hot sand feels great on naked skin, as does the cool water. The other two nudist beaches are Cobblers Beach and Obelisk Beach at Middle Head. To get to Lady's Bay, walk over the hill from Camp Cove at Watsons Bay and climb down a ladder. We recommend you do that part with your clothes on. Further towards the CBD at Tamarama, or 'Glamarama' as it's been dubbed, you'll see more G-strings than bare buttocks but, still, remember to wax.

Art

For a more obvious sensory tour, start at the **Art Gallery of NSW** *(Art Gallery Rd)* where the Royal Blind Society sculpture *Mobius Sea*, by Richard Goodwin, feels like a giant mass of limbs, says Nicholas Gleeson of Vision Australia, who also loves the squat, brass pig in Macquarie St, near Parliament House, its snout burnished gold from being rubbed for luck.

"When I feel a sculpture, I also think about the place it sits – near a busy roadside, or in a quiet park – and wonder about what it would be like to live there day and night, watching people both rich and poor, and happy and troubled, passing by," he says. Among his other favourite haptic art experiences are the two lions guarding the gates of Centennial Park and a Henry Moore sculpture of a woman located between the Opera House and the Art Gallery of NSW. Gleeson prefers to discover larger sculptures not only by reaching out to touch them but also by climbing all around them. It's probably frowned upon by park rangers but, as he says, they have to catch you first. (He's climbed Mt Kilimanjaro, so the rangers would want to be fairly fit.)

At **Bradfield Park**, in the tiny north shore suburb of Lavender Bay, sculptor Clary Akon has fashioned an Australian terrier in the heritage rockery garden that is so lifelike you expect a wagging tail. It sits on top of the Jessie Broomfield Memorial Dog Drinking Fountain, first built in 1953.

Akon encourages people to touch the sculpture, and run their hands through the cool water of the drinking fountain. "Like all art sculpture, it is aspirational: our innate drive to express the human condition in which we exist," he says. "A sculptor moulds these aspirations and sets them in time and space. The static grace of a sculpture serves as an anchor point in our mind: an illusion of permanence where the reality is of flux. Once in a while someone reaches out to pat a bronze terrier and makes this same connection."

Keep walking down Lavender St and into **Clark Park** to find a bronze teapot entitled *A Nite to Remember* by Edward Randall Moss. It is engraved with the names of Hollywood stars and songs, and offers more opportunity to explore by fingertip. Nearby, some of Peter Kingston's sculptural series *Hidden Treasures* are set among the plants along the boardwalk. Walk from Luna Park until you reach Lavender Bay Wharf, and then look right. You'll see cherished comic characters in miniature, including Australian icons Blinky Bill, Snugglepot and Cuddlepie, which send thrills through hands and hearts.

In a city as artistically and culturally diverse as Sydney, it's good think laterally about touch. At the tiny **All Hand Made Gallery** *(252 Bronte Rd, Waverley; 9386 4099)* potter and curator Helen Stephens has applied her own artist's eye in choosing a range of work from some of Australia's leading ceramics artists to mesmerise both the eyes and the fingertips. Kaye Rice's beakers, made from iron-rich clay she digs herself in Mudgee; Patsy Healy's three-dimensional nature vase with bird; and Sandy Lockwood's bubbled, salt-glazing all convey stories best read by touch.

Also handle the merchandise at Sydney's slowest shops, including carefully woven fabrics like the silken threads used by designer and cloth artist Akira Isogawa, which can feel very therapeutic (as long as you show some restraint when handling your own credit card!).

...rr

ug

bunu

bamu

guiga

mamb

mugag

budjor

guman

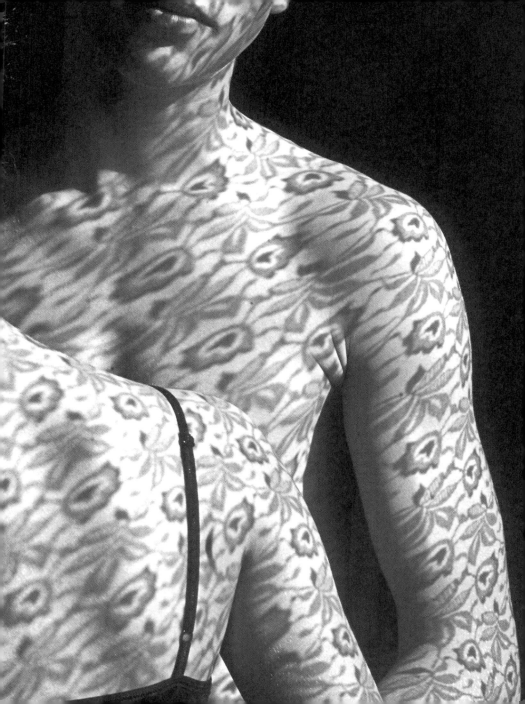

Community

Touchy Feely

There are few better ways of feeling connected with your community than through volunteering, and you can gain a lot from giving something back: peace of mind, perspective and even a rise in your own self-esteem.

There are many ways to spend goodwill beyond the traditional selflessness of working in an op shop or delivering Meals on Wheels, as noble as they are. Volunteering can be anything from helping a refugee family settle into their new life by visiting them at home once a week and teaching elderly people how to use computers to weeding a patch of bushland for one day only or sharpening your stand-up skills at a home for the disabled.

Whatever it is, giving a little of yourself for someone else's good is a fantastic way to become engaged in the community – and you'll find out that the old cliché about giving being better than receiving is absolutely true.

Your skills can be put to good use somewhere in the world of volunteer work: the system is amazingly well organised these days, and a good place to start looking for opportunities is www.volunteering.com.au.

Another great site is www.goodcompany .com.au, an organisation that has been operating in Sydney since 2003 and aims to team up the specific skills of young professionals with the needs of not-for-profits. Register your interest and expertise, and you'll receive a regular wish list collating the wants and needs of worthwhile charities throughout Sydney.

Community Gardens

It's difficult to find the Randwick Community Organic Garden, a dip in the corner of Paine Reserve, next door to Randwick Boys High School. But then you notice the bees buzzing between passionflowers and yellow broccolini blossom, flitting butterflies and birds twittering – and realise life is happening right here. Neat and abundant rows of beans, artichokes and other fabulous-looking vegetables, plus citrus trees and beds of herbs, fill the site; along one side stands a line of compost bins.

Community gardens are dotted all over Sydney, some in the most unlikely of spots, in pocket-sized local parks and the gardens of disused Housing Commission houses. With apartment living becoming the norm, and neighbourliness on the wane, community gardens can do a lot for both body and soul. They're a chance to get to know like-minded folk, work up a sweat and get some soil under the fingernails. And there's great satisfaction taking home the fruits (and vegetables) of your labours.

Some gardens work as allotments, with members taking responsibility for each plot; at others, everyone just mucks in for the greater good. The first community garden in Sydney was started in 1985 in the grounds of Rozelle Hospital – now, like the uncertain climate we live in, they're appearing and disappearing with alarming regularity around the city. For more information, visit www .communityfoods.org.au or www.commun itygarden.org.au. ∎

Secret Garden

A friend was looking for Wendy Whiteley's garden around Milsons Point one day, but the people she asked for directions had never heard of it. She got the distinct impression they knew exactly where it was but preferred to keep it to themselves. You can't blame them, really. This slice of Railcorp land off Clark Park, alongside where the trains sleep at night, is one of those places that suddenly makes you want to play hide-and-seek or start exploring – a place ribboned with stairways and narrow pathways and a massive clump of bamboo that's good for the soul and has the miraculous effect of turning you into a six-year-old again.

The secret garden was covered in lantana until Wendy, widow of the artist Brett Whiteley, got her hands on it several years ago and started clearing away the weeds and unearthing old basins and lawnmowers, which now appear as ready-made sculpture. Underneath it all the soil was rich and ready for new life, which Whiteley and local volunteers provide. One of the gardeners, an ex-lifesaver from Newquay in England, shows us around, pointing out the lemon tree, dripping with fruit, the pink grapefruit, mandarins and cumquats, the herb garden, the strawberries and the quince trees. "It's all here for the taking," he says, and it seems everyone treats that philosophy with the respect it deserves. The local council, he says, brings down mulch and carts away the clippings.

He tells us about the local resident who works in a nursery and donates leftover plants to the garden. "We plant everything we've got – it's all a bit of an experiment," which only adds to the haphazard charm of the place – the geraniums alongside the grevillea, the nasturtiums and roses near the palms and tree ferns. "We're trying to plant more natives to encourage birds and native animals – there were some tawny frogmouths here recently, and there are always blue-tongue lizards around."

The garden, which has given solace to Wendy Whiteley since the death of Brett and their daughter, Arkie, keeps growing as more sections get cleared. It also attracts a lovely mix of human life – little girls in school uniform worried that their friends will get lost ("Come back here, now…please"), couples getting married ("All we ask for is a few plants as payment," says the gardener), picnicking families and someone who just wants a quiet and magical place to read, on a bench made from an old sleeper donated by the railways.

I love the feel of...

Do

IN THE PURSUIT OF SLOW

NURTURE
Take Care of Yourself

-------------------------------- • --------------------------------

" NOTHING CAN CURE THE SOUL BUT THE SENSES, JUST AS
NOTHING CAN CURE THE SENSES BUT THE SOUL. "

Oscar Wilde

nurture

motion

travel

small

play

gather

Ideally, we wouldn't forget about ourselves. We're not talking about the me-me-me infatuation of the aspirational generation. Rather, the need to nurture oneself and take care of body and soul.

"Although we're all different and although we all have different goals, aspirations and dreams, it's hard to imagine anything more important in life than our health and happiness," says Dr Tim Sharp, founder of Sydney's Happiness Institute. "But if we want to be healthier or happier, we need to look after ourselves."

Becoming mired in a fast-paced city lifestyle can leave us with very little time to achieve that goal, he says. Yet the good news is that simply slowing down and savouring all that life – and the city – has to offer will go a long way towards improving our overall health and happiness.

Lift your spirits: drifting on incense or rising to the lofty ceilings of one of the city's formal houses of worship. Find peace at the local art gallery. Connect with nature in the abundant parks, coastal tracks and beaches. What does it matter if the place you seek out for yourself is a spa, a temple, a salon or a cookery class? "The ultimate goal is the same. Everyone desires health and happiness," Sharp says. The trick is to slow down long enough to find it.

Indulgence

When the going gets tough, more and more Sydneysiders are going to a spa. It's about pampering, and life balance, but also about getting in touch with both the physical and the metaphysical. On a more superficial level, it can also be about pure indulgence, a laugh with friends or a special treat because…well, do you need a reason?

Salons and Spas

Step off chaotic King St into the **Buddha Bar Healing Clinic** *(365 King St, Newtown; 9517 9725)* and you can feel the energy change around you almost immediately. Bamboo screens and Buddhas create a sanctuary of calm. While there are four interior treatment rooms, it's the outdoor area – with its dark deck and red cushions, bamboo brush and gazebos built around an avocado tree – that works best for unkinking those physical and psychic knots. Treatments range from aromatherapy, massage and Chinese cupping to counselling and Reiki. The clinic, which owner Kim Williams describes as a community space, also offers meditation classes and drumming workshops.

At **Spa Chakra** *(Woolloomooloo Bay; 9368 0888)*, valet parking and beverages are included in every treatment but if you feel like spending more after your facial or massage treatment, you can have a tarot reading, an appointment with their in-house naturopath or a session with a GP who specialises in anti-ageing medicine.

If you're stressed and in need of some urgent TLC, look no further than the **Centre of Attention** *(4 Anderson St, Double Bay; 9327 5572; www.centreofattention.com.au)*, which will make you feel like royalty the moment you arrive. Heritage Healers teas, custom blended to your body type, are served with chocolates and offered for nix at the end of your treatments. If you do a standard day package, you'll chow down on a silver-service light lunch and they'll also organise a limo to drop you home if you live in the eastern suburbs.

When it comes to all-out pampering, **Gillian Adams** *(1356 Pacific Hwy, Turramurra; www.gillianadams.com.au; 9488 9944)* wrote the book. Unlike many salons that like call to themselves spas, this is the real deal as evidenced by the large oxygenated Aquamedic marble pool straight out of the pages of the *Great Gatsby*. All treatments include a dip in the pool, which has therapeutic massaging jets, as well as a gourmet lunch.

Sage Beauty *(292 Campbell Pde, North Bondi; 9130 7064)* – run on green power and jammed with organic treatments and products – is devoted to eco lifestyle. Owner Junia Kerr, a homeopath for 15 years, oversees treatments that range from healing facials that begin with a sage footbath ("It helps ground people") to naturopathic consultations, advice on fertility and even referrals to a midwife and doulas. Sage Beauty uses plant wax for its tealight candles and biodegradable plastic bags for waste, and sells natural cleaning products, eco lamps and Dr Hauschka organic skincare products.

A 'high touch facial' at **Aveda** *(17 Oxford St, Paddington; 9380 5550)* includes a scalp massage that will probably relax you into a state of jelly-like euphoria. It's part of the Elemental Nature Radiance Facial package, which basically means the therapist doesn't just apply a mask and leave you staring at the ceiling for quarter of an hour. This salon offers some of the best treatments around, and you'll have help here with the entire Aveda range, all made with pure flower and plant essences.

Step inside the **Inspa Wellness Retreat** *(331 Rocky Point Rd, Sans Souci; 9529 8922)* and you are immediately calmed by soft hues and light-timber features complemented by Japanese antique furniture. The surroundings are made specifically for quiet, meditative relax-ation. A white-pebbled pathway leads to the retreat's Zen garden, pagoda and courtyard where the soothing sounds of water gently spill over the landscape. Owner Kara Miller is a qualified aromatherapist and reflexologist with qualifications in Chinese Facial Diagnosis and Reiki. A percentage of all promotional retail sales are donated to the McGrath Foundation for Breast Cancer Nurses.

Aroma Ki's *(Pittwater Rd, Collaroy Beach; 9982 2446)* Rasul mud treatment (incorporating Dead Sea mud, organic and biodynamic herbs and aromatherapy essences) is a cleansing body treatment. The only Rasul bath experience in Sydney, it starts with a therapist covering you in mud, after which you are put in a chamber of dry heat until the mud dries, steamed for 20 minutes, and then washed under automatic showers. You can then choose a massage or facial to finish your treatment.

Seaside Sanatorium

Immortalised by artist Jeffrey Smart in his series of works depicting Sydneysiders reclining on the decking, Wylie's Baths *(Neptune St, Coogee)* is an inspiration for all who visit. Established by super swimmer Henry Alexander Wylie in 1907, Wylies is built on a rock shelf, affords spectacular views over Coogee Beach and is one of a series of charming pools cut into the base of our seaside cliffs.

The decking, precariously suspended and framed by a balustrade with an iconic chequerboard pattern, is not quite the original. A kiosk has been added and you can now get a massage or do some yoga. What hasn't changed is how much fun it is to dive into the huge pool and feel like you're in a fish tank. The water is flushed by the tide twice a day, and you are at one with lichen, seaweed and tiny, brightly coloured fish.

For a day at Wylie's, take a sketchbook, a hat and towel and soak up the view, the salty air and the ambience. In sunny weather, a more perfect way to spend some time in Sydney is almost unimaginable.

Why sweat your way through a boring, eardrum-splitting aerobics class when there are other more mindful and scintillating ways to tone up the body beautiful? Begone chain-style fitness networks where sweat-suited exercisers are packed into cavernous halls like proverbial sardines and blasted with music not of their choice. Enter more exotic, gentle or traditional ways of paying attention to one's wellness and physique.

Brazilian rhythms fill the training room as sleekly muscled men and women put their bodies through what seems like a mixture of a martial-arts display and a Rio dance festival. They are here for **Capoeira** *(www.capoeiracre.com/oz.htm; 0414 745 161)*. "Capoeira is a full body exercise that pushes you to the limits; from improving overall fitness, strength, coordination, flexibility and agility, as well as being able to relax the mind through song," explains practitioner John Rosiello. "It is a sport and martial art that knows no barriers."

Rosiello loves it because "it is the music; the drums that beat deep like a heart beat, the sharp claps of the Capoeiristas watching your every move with the mesmerising sound of the Berimbau resonating and controlling the rhythm and tempo of the game." The class culture is also different from many other martial arts, made special by the pulsating Brazilian music, and there's a good mix of men and women.

Flamenco is about rhythm, music, passion and exploding colour. It's also about footwork, arm movements and wrist work, and that can be difficult to get right. No matter. **Diana Reyes** *(585b King St, Newtown; 9557 1825)* has been teaching flamenco for nearly two decades and reckons she can make even the clumsiest beginner become at least mildly proficient within a year of lessons. "Flamenco is my passion; I love the dance and I love the rhythm," she says. "You are using your body as an instrument; your feet as percussion." Flamenco is great for fitness, posture and coordination, adds Reyes.

Whoever heard of a health club being described as elegant? With its saltwater Greco-style pool overseen by a Russian swimming champion; luxe day spa where you can get a detoxifying seaweed wrap, a scalp massage or even teeth whitening; and a crèche where untidy children can be hidden away, that is exactly what **Temple of the Body & Soul** *(100 New South Head Rd, Edgecliff; www.templeof bodysoul.com.au; 9362 9988)* achieves.

The Temple has been designed especially for women, and club membership is capped to avoid sweaty overcrowding. But, thankfully, you can still visit casually. Leave the Merc out front – there's valet parking – and pop in to see the life coach, have a steam or sauna, work out with a personal trainer or try a private Pilates class. The décor is lush, lush, lush. Think creams and caramels, Buddha heads, low lighting and lots of fluffy white towels.

For body fitness on the inside, visit **Natural Progression Nutrition & Health** *(Shop 81, Gould St, Bondi Beach; 9130 2080)* where owner Debbie Muller has filled a tiny space with the best natural and specialist products around, from chemical-free skincare to nutritional supplements. If it's high quality, or hard to get, you'll find it here. There's even a herbal dispensary with prepared homeopathics and fresh organic vegies next door. ∎

One Perfect Day

Plan your own nurturing day. Begin with dry body brushing, with a soft-bristle brush – use smooth, upward strokes – then shower with a body wash scented with your favourite smell. Gently stretch every limb, perhaps to music, then stroll somewhere scenic. Take time for a leisurely breakfast before a spa or salon appointment, ideally for something pampering. In the afternoon, pay a visit to one of Sydney's most beautiful buildings or churches, like the State Library or St Mary's Cathedral. Stop at an organic outlet (see page 93) for supplies. At home, prepare a gigantic salad full of organic vegetables, seeds and nuts and then treat yourself to an aromatherapy bath. Add lavender for healing, or neroli to lift the spirit. Feeling more in tune with yourself and your surrounds, spend some time outdoors, gazing at the stars before turning in.

Natural Therapies

Ancient, Oriental arts are enjoying a surge in popularity in Sydney as more and more of us step out of the fast lane and into a more balanced, appreciative space.

The low-key **Wholistic Medical Centre** *(1st floor, 17 Randle St, Surry Hills; 9211 3811)* was Australia's first and is promoted by loyal regulars spreading their good news. Traditional Chinese Medicine practitioner Shona Barker is much sought-after for her gentle and effective treatments and soothing manner. Naturopath and author Deborah Cooper and osteopath Tim Hulbert are also leaders in their respective fields. A different blend of herbal tea is always on offer in the waiting room, as well as alternative magazines and lists of classes and contacts.

A cross between a day spa, a health retreat and a medical clinic, **Equilibrium** *(11-13 Avalon Pde, Avalon; 9973 2904)* aims to address all your health needs: physical, mental and spiritual. Begin the day with a yoga class, then move onto a consultation with a nutritionist, psychotherapist, acupuncturist or GP, and end your session with a soothing massage. In a way, it's like checking into a health spa for the day. Choosing what you need is easy because life coach and counsellor Christina Brimage is on hand and will help you identify what you want and how to get it.

Learn how to slow down and smile. One of Sydney's leading positive psychology practices, the **Happiness Institute** *(Suite 401, 74 Pitts St; www.thehappinessinstitute.com; 9221 3306)* is at the cutting edge of international developments in using positive thinking and practices to improve the quality of our lives. Director Tim Sharp's nickname is Dr Happy,

and his mission is to get people to understand they need to work to achieve happiness; it doesn't always come naturally.

We shouldn't really be telling you about the **Body Therapy Clinic** *(2/2 Moore Ave, Lindfield; 9880 9499)*. It's only a little massage place run by husband-and-wife team Iris and Mark Wainer and, next time we need a shoulder corrected or a neck de-tensed, we probably won't be able to get in. But the truth is Mark can de-stress anybody and everybody, and Iris teaches yoga classes that are guaranteed to realign your workstation-addled posture. They carry such a sense of calm and nurturing that you just give yourself over to their capable hands until they hand your green tea at the end of the session.

Sit in on the **Laughing Class** *(www.laughterclubsnsw.com)* at 10am every Sunday morning at Bondi Pavilion, and you start off feeling a little ridiculous. Laughing for no reason with a bunch of strangers? Surely you have better things to do on the weekend – or maybe not. Noni Gove, of NSW Laughter Clubs, says laughter makes you less stressed, more self-confident and can not only help give you abs of steel but lower your risk of disease. Who's laughing now?

Learning to meditate can be the best starting point for slowing down. Join the ohming throngs at the **Dhammakaya Meditation Centre** *(117 Homebush Rd, Strathfield; www.dhammakaya.org.au; 9742 3031)* located in the tranquil hilltop bushland of Berowa Waters. Alternatively, Sydney's **Buddhist Centre** *(24 Enmore Rd, Newtown; 9519 0440)* offers weekend meditation retreats suitable for absolute beginners. Or you can try experienced Sydney teacher **Stuart Mackay** *(www.peaceatwork.com)*.

Art Class

Admiring the work of Brett Whiteley or John Olsen in the Art Gallery of NSW is one thing. Taking a class that may at least turn you into someone who makes meaningful marks on a canvas is a more proactive way to exercise your creativity. I decide to try a life drawing class. The room is warm and dimly lit, except for the podium where the model will sit under spotlight. There are chairs all around, portraits on the wall and, overall, the setting lives up to the life-drawing scenes I've seen in movies, except I'm not in a romantic French garrison, with a guy in a beret splashing paint on a canvas. There is one arty-looking guy, complete with kerchief and black clothes, among the mixture of students – including mums and businesspeople.

As we all wait, sketchpads and pencils at the ready, there is a general air of expectation and a certain nervousness, perhaps because of the etiquette involved in drawing a nude. No one wants to seem anything but professional. The model's arrival is greeted with 10 pairs of eyes. He's about 23, and dressed in jeans and a T-shirt. He makes eye contact with the teacher, but then he's out the back to return wearing just a robe, which he removes unselfconsciously.

He's a terrific specimen: very muscular and firm, with a prominent nose and curly hair. He strikes a pose, sitting with his arms behind his back. "Two minute sketches," calls the teacher, and suddenly it's a race, with the sound of pencils scraping across paper. "Change!" A new pose – kneeling with his arms extended. Capturing the model's form is harder than I think: everyone draws very intensely but it is very relaxing. I am totally focused and involved, almost like meditation.

I leave clutching a selection of sketches that will make lovely portraits with more work, and the memory of an evening spent with a model who was fairly easy on the eye.

Try your own life-drawing class at the Art House Hotel *(275 Pitt St; www.art househotel.com.au; 9284 1200)* on Monday nights. They even give you a glass of wine to loosen your nerves. The building itself also has a pretty arty pedigree – designed in 1830, it was a school of education and then arts before falling derelict by the 1920s. In 1999 it was restored as a venue to encourage vibrant arts such as cabaret, burlesque, jazz and, of course, amateur artists.

MICKEY HAWKES

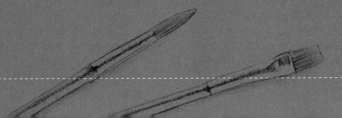

Lost in Music

The usual reaction when anyone finds out you've taken up a musical instrument is "You're so brave." Or else, a little less frequently, "I wish I could do that." You can't help feeling that, secretly, they're also thinking, "That's ridiculous – who's she trying to fool?"

Yes, taking up a violin decades after everyone else has given it up does seem slightly crazy – there's absolutely no chance of ever being a concert violinist. But that's never been the point. For anyone who suffered music lessons as a child, and hated practising (as I did, when I learnt the piano for a year or two), it's a revelation to find out that music teachers can actually be friendly and make lessons enjoyable, and that playing scales, when you're in the right frame of mind, can take on a meditative quality rather than be an outright chore.

As a kid, playing music was the equivalent of "Are we there yet?" on a long car journey; as an adult, I discover a patience I never knew I had. I love the violin's unpredictability – some days, in my hands, it can

sound almost beautiful, and at other times excruciating. Nine years after my first lesson, I realise the violin fits perfectly into the living-in-the-moment philosophy that shapes my whole life – the end result is completely irrelevant; the process is all that matters. There's no answer when people ask me how far I want to go with it.

The lowdown: taking up a musical instrument doesn't need to be a major commitment either time-wise or in a financial sense. There's no need to fork out and buy one – most instruments can be hired by the month until you decide whether it's really your thing (contact music shops for more details). As for teachers, you can ask at your local music shop or contact the Sydney Conservatorium of Music *(www .music.usyd.edu.au)*, but don't be afraid to approach musicians after a concert or gig. Many teach music part-time, and are only too happy to take on a new student; those that don't can often point you in the right direction.

LETA KEENS

Class Action

Another great way to nurture yourself and reconnect with your spirit is to indulge in a hobby – anything from dance to spice appreciation.

Cooking

The secret to any great meal is simplicity, fresh organic ingredients, love and intuition, according to Maria Bernardis, the founder of **Greekalicious** *(www.greekalicious.com.au)*. Maria spent her childhood on the Greek Island of Psara helping her grandmother cook and acquiring the culinary wisdom she now shares with Sydneysiders. Caring about what you cook with (meaning your ingredients and your heart) is crucial for enjoying and sharing meals, is her philosophy. Classes are run regularly in Paddington and range from the food of Crete to aphrodisiacs. Pass the ouzo.

If your idea of health, wealth or simple pleasure is a seafood banquet, spend some time at the school that teaches Sydneysiders how to make use of the natural bounty from their harbour. At **Sydney Seafood School** *(Sydney Fish Markets, Pyrmont; www.sydney fishmarket.com.au),* chefs like Matthew Moran and Damien Pignolet teach students how to prepare, cook and eat everything from pipis to sea snails. As fishmongers present the freshest catches, your mouth waters imagining which of these you'll be learning to stir-fry, stuff or barbecue today. You'll need to book early for the most popular class, seafood BBQ, where you learn how an afternoon in the sun with a cold beer or sauvignon blanc can be more relaxed and indulgent than just throwing a few prawns on the barbie.

If you don't know your coriander from your galangal, the chances are you need to spice up your life. You could run for politics or taking up pole dancing. But may we suggest a Spice Appreciation class instead, at the home of herbs and spices in Sydney, **Herbie's Spices** *(745 Darling St, Rozelle; 9555 6035).* Classes are limited to 10 people so you're not afraid to ask questions. Besides demystifying flavours, you'll get ideas for creating inspired food whether you are single, part of a family or an already knowledgeable gourmet.

Dance

Want to be a bejewelled, exotic Goddess? Watch a bellydancer with an emerald in her navel, her pelvis seemingly rotating independently of her anatomy and it looks, well, if not easy, then at least doable. But learning the basic movements (hip circles, forward and backward figure-eights, hip bumps, drops and lifts, belly rolls, diaphragm circles, shimmy, snake arms) is, whew, challenging. At **Sydney Community College** *(www.sydneycommunitycol lege.com.au)* you can try out dance styles including Egyptian, Turkish or Lebanese and then practice them in the privacy of your own lounge room. Bellydancing really is a hobby that will help you contemplate your navel. The college also runs classes in film and video, photography, jewellery-making, textiles and fashion, writing, music and handcrafts.

Surfing

Ever since Hawaiians jumped on wooden planks and took to the ocean, surfing has been cool. In Sydney, it's a religion. And, if you know how to do it, well, welcome to the brother-...or sisterhood. **Manly Surf School** *(North Steyne Surf Club, Manly; www.manlysurfschool.com)* is the most well known, although you will find others around the city. Why surf? Says motivational therapist, northern beaches boy and surfer Glen Pattison: "You get out in the waves on a warm, clear day and it's just you and the roar of the surf. No hassles. No mobile phones. And then, if you're lucky, the best ride on top of a gnarly wave."

Learning

Hear an astronomer talk about "dark matter", learn how the sick were treated in the time of Hippocrates or let an architect draw you into the visionary world of the Sydney Opera House architect Jørn Utzon. **Sydney Talks** *(www.syd neytalks.com.au)*, held at some of the city's most beautiful buildings (from the State Library to the Powerhouse Museum), are a great way to be entertained and get an education.

Permaculture

We have seen the future and it is permaculture – "the harmonious integration of landscape and people providing their food, energy, shelter and other needs in a sustainable way," says the Permaculture Institute. In other words, it's about working with nature, not against it, and as a part of the community. There are permaculture groups springing up like fresh seeds, many connected to community gardens. **Permaculture North** *(258 Pacific Hwy, Lindfield; 1300 887 145)*, formed in 1992, is a diverse group with an amazing array of skills in energy and water conservation plus permaculture design, as well as beginners learning about healthier living. There are regular talks and visits, backyard working bees and skills trading.

Acting

It might not be Tinseltown but acting, or writing a script, or directing a script, or selling that damn script, is a topic of some fervour in Sydney. If you'd like to tread the boards, try a short course in pretending to be someone you are not. One of the most prestigious acting schools is the **Actors Centre Australia** *(241 Devonshire St, Surry Hills; 9310 4077)*. It was established in 1986 within a suitably dramatic venue – an 1880 heritage-listed church. The Centre's Skills Studio offers short courses in TV presenting, stand-up comedy, singing, improvisation, audition techniques, script work and accents, as well as acting for camera and the stage.

Music

If you've always wanted to sing with a group, there are several community choirs catering to all levels, with **Sydney Philharmonia Choirs** *(www.sydneyphilharmonia.com.au)* at the top of the heap. If you've always wanted to sing, full stop, but have the kind of voice that had your teacher pleading with you to mime during school concerts, sign up for the 10-week **Tone Deaf Clinic** *(Music Practice; Surry Hills; www.musicpractice.com.au)*. You'll never be scared of singing 'Happy Birthday' again.

HAPPINESS IS AS A BUTTERFLY WHICH, WHEN PURSUED, IS ALWAYS BEYOND OUR GRASP, BUT WHICH IF YOU WILL SIT DOWN QUIETLY, MAY ALIGHT UPON YOU.

Nathaniel Hawthorne

MOTION
Ways to Go

---•---

"
SLOW DOWN, YOU MOVE TOO FAST.
YOU GOT TO MAKE THE MORNING LAST.
JUST KICKING DOWN THE COBBLESTONES.
LOOKING FOR FUN AND FEELIN'
GROOVY…LA-LA-LA-LAA-LAA-LAA…FEELIN' GROOVY.
"

Simon and Garfunkel

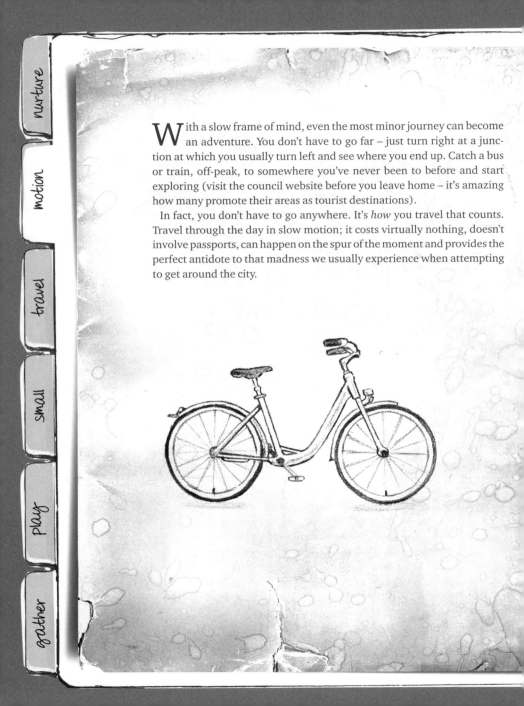

nurture

motion

travel

small

play

gather

W ith a slow frame of mind, even the most minor journey can become an adventure. You don't have to go far – just turn right at a junction at which you usually turn left and see where you end up. Catch a bus or train, off-peak, to somewhere you've never been to before and start exploring (visit the council website before you leave home – it's amazing how many promote their areas as tourist destinations).

In fact, you don't have to go anywhere. It's *how* you travel that counts. Travel through the day in slow motion; it costs virtually nothing, doesn't involve passports, can happen on the spur of the moment and provides the perfect antidote to that madness we usually experience when attempting to get around the city.

By Foot

Naturally, the **Bondi to Clovelly** cliff walk, which started as a state project during the 30s, is an absolute must. The only problem is that half of Sydney agrees, so sometimes it'll feel like you're on George St. Never mind; join the joggers, the dog walkers and the amblers, and take it at your own pace, stopping at Bronte for a dip (the baths were built in 1887) or at Waverley Cemetery, the graveyard with the best views in Australia – how Sydney can you get? – and where such notables as Henry Lawson and Dorothea Mackellar ("I love a sunburnt country") are buried.

For something less frenetic, head in the opposite direction from Bondi for the 3km **Dover Heights to Watson's Bay** walk. You'll come across patches of remnant vegetation along the way, including a hanging swamp with rushes and grasses at Diamond Bay Reserve, which is also home to geckos, water skinks and delicate skinks. A hanging swamp is a special type of wetland usually found in

places with poor drainage on cliff edges and hillsides. Water seeps up through the ground and is caught in layers of sandstone, creating damp conditions perfect for ferns and mosses, which then trap sediment and leaves to form a wonderfully rich wetland ecosystem.

The **Manly to Spit Bridge** walk, which takes about four hours and isn't too taxing, is the perfect way to take in the harbour as you follow the shoreline and pass Aboriginal sites (there's a midden at Fisher Bay), beaches, bushland, parks and even subtropical rainforest. Near Clontarf Point is a stand of Sydney red gums – the pink-grey bark of which flakes off in spring to reveal a fresh new orange layer underneath. There's a Grotto Point lighthouse, which was built in 1910 and looks a bit like a Greek chapel from a distance.

It's not only in the 21st century that planners make major errors with their roads. One of our earliest was a complete disaster, but is now a great place for a walk if you're up

Ripper Rail Route

OK, so it's not the *Orient Express*, but the Metro Light Rail *(www.metrolightrail.com .au)* reveals much of Sydney as it weaves from Central through Chinatown and Darling Harbour before heading off towards the fish markets (jump off on the way back to pick up dinner), Wentworth Park's greyhound racecourse, Glebe and Lilyfield.

The stop at Jubilee Park is a great place to start exploring the Glebe Point area. The Light Rail goes between Central and Lilyfield from 6am to 11pm (midnight on Friday and Saturday), but round the clock daily between Central and, we hate to say it, Star City Casino.

for a bit of history and adventure, and have a few days to spare. The **Great North Rd** connects Sydney with the Hunter Valley and was built by convict labour. It was completed in 1836, by which time it was already a write-off as coastal steamers were the preferred mode of transport to the Hunter. A 43km-long section remains undeveloped and intact, and contains the oldest surviving stone bridges in mainland Australia. It starts at Wiseman's Ferry and heads north to Mount Manning (near Bucketty) – it's also great for a bike ride.

The **National Parks Association of NSW** *(www.npansw.org.au)* organises bushwalks virtually every day of the year, for everyone from the sloth to Indiana Jones, from gentle strolls to a trudge through quicksand. But you needn't wait to stretch your legs in bush; you can stay completely within the urban jungle and still get away from it all.

One of the nicest inner-city walks is along **Bourke St** at Surry Hills, which, after a few road closures, has been transformed into a very peaceful patch. Start at Taylor Square and meander your way slowly to Cleveland St, stopping in at **Bourke Street Bakery** *(633 Bourke St)* for a coffee, a treat and a rest on the way.

A couple of detours are essential – one to the Brett Whiteley studio (see page 56), where the painter lived and worked for a few years before his death in 1992, and the other to McElhone Place, Sydney's sweetest street. It's tiny – only wide enough for pedestrians, bicycles and the odd cat – and is an oasis of frangipani, oleanders, bougainvillea, roses and gardenias, all planted in pots by the green-thumbed and fiercely proud residents of this little enclave. It wins the Greening of Sydney Award every year, hardly giving any other street a chance.

By Lead

Treat you and your dog to a new walk – you'll both enjoy a change of scenery. As long as you keep your dog on a leash, you can venture to most parks (council websites and www .petsplayground.com.au denote which and when).

A picturesque place for a decent run, leash-free (at certain times during the day) is Rushcutters Bay Park, between Elizabeth Bay and Darling Point. It's where all the big boats moor before the start of the Sydney to Hobart Yacht Race. The park is the local meeting spot for dogs and their owners, who all seem to be the best of friends.

Just down the road and equally picturesque, but smaller and quieter, is Yarranabbe Park *(New Beach Rd)* at Darling Point. While the mutt's stretching, sit on the sandstone wall and watch schools of little fish swimming near the shore.

Rover can practise his doggy paddle at Rowland Reserve *(Pittwater Rd)*, Bayview, and dry off with a jolly good run through a huge grassy area. You can have an unfettered stroll on the beach at Sirius Cove, Mosman, during the week or on weekend evenings.

5. Great North Road

Manly to Spit Bridge   1.

2.

Dover Heights
Watson's Bay

Bourke Street
Surry Hills   4.

Bondi to
Clovelly   3.

N
W   E
S

By Pedal

It's a winning combination on all fronts: two wheels and no motor means you won't be adding to greenhouse gases, you'll be expending energy and getting fitter, plus you'll be going slowly enough to actually enjoy what's around you. Cycling has to be the transport mode for the 21st century.

Sydney's not the most bike-friendly city, but there are an increasing number of clearly marked cycleways, often in the most unlikely places. You'll find good bike maps on the RTA website *(www.rta.nsw.gov.au)*.

One of the best rides to start with, mainly because it's easy all the way and is only 17km-long, starts at Tempe station. The Cooks River Cycleway follows the course of the river through sleepy suburbs and through parks you've never seen before. Yes, it does cross a few main roads, where you'll have to keep your wits about you. It ends at Olympic Park, which is itself criss-crossed by cycleways, so if you're feeling energetic you can keep pedalling. Otherwise, you can catch the train home from Olympic Park station.

Another easy river ride starts at Parramatta Regional Park, and follows the Parramatta River past some historic spots – one in the general vicinity is the Yaralla Estate, containing an Italianate mansion by Edmund Blacket and John Sulman, Sydney's most famous 19th-century architects, and Australia's first squash court, built in the 20s for the Prince of Wales' visit. After 15km, you'll arrive at the Kissing Point Ferry, on the Circular Quay to Parramatta ferry route. By the way, bikes travel free on all Sydney ferries and off-peak trains; during peak hour, you'll need to buy a child's train ticket for your bicycle.

Once you've got your fitness levels up, have a crack at the 26km Centennial Park to South Head ride. After a bit of a spin around the park, you'll head towards Double Bay, 'Heartbreak Hill', Vaucluse House, Watsons Bay, Bondi Beach and back to Centennial Park. It's one of the most picturesque rides around and it's tempting to keep your eyes on the harbour views rather than the road.

By Gosh

The walk up through the Rocks to Sydney Observatory just before 8pm on Sunday is quiet. Almost everything is closed, a bus taking ghost tours sits outside the Argyle Centre, fairy lights glitter in the trees along Argyle St. Even the Observatory itself is quiet, except for a group of around 20 – tourists and locals, schoolchildren and singles, young couples on a date – standing around in the dark. When the doors don't open on the dot of 8pm, a few people start getting impatient. But what are a few minutes when we will be dealing with light years inside?

We're split into two groups. We go with Paul Hancock, a researcher in astrophysics, who is as enthusiastic as you would expect from someone who spends his life looking at the sky. Before we head up to the serious stuff – the actual telescope – we're left to look around the museum. It's too late at night to concentrate on instruments and we're more taken with the observing couch, a moth-eaten leather contraption on rollers used by astronomers when they had to lie on their backs and stare for hours through a telescope eyepiece.

It doesn't take long before Paul leads us up into the first copper-lined dome, which holds a telescope from the 1800s, and tells us not to "hang back on difficult or stupid questions". No one asks anything for a while, until a boy, about 10, asks why the light globes near the telescope are red. A bit of nervous laughter ensues, but it's not a silly question. With regular bulbs it would take our eyes too long to adjust to the dark night sky. Paul presses a button and a section of the roof slowly starts to roll open, like a garage door. He swivels the narrow slit around until it faces a sliver of relatively clear sky, and lines up the old telescope. After months of clear skies, there's heavy cloud cover, and the moon and stars keep coming and going. He points the telescope at a flickering light, and we all take turns to look at Betelgeuse, a red giant 427 light years away and 1000 times the size of the sun. Figures like that can start to make you feel a bit woozy. "If it looks a bit jumpy, it's either the cloud cover or because you've knocked the telescope," says Paul.

On a clear night, we'd be able to look at the moon and Mars and everything, but tonight we go down to the planetarium and lie in the darkened room on beanbags under a giant umbrella pinpricked with the southern skies.

Paul points out constellations and talks about the Milky Way, Van Allen belt and the number of stars in the sky, and it's almost as if we've really seen it all. We go back upstairs to the second domed chamber, which was built in the 1870s after the time-ball tower went up and blocked a huge section of sky from the original dome. In this second space, a much newer telescope is in place, but we still can't see much – clouds have won the night. But it doesn't matter – as we make our way back down Observatory Hill, the car tail lights seem brighter and faster and somehow just a little bit insignificant.
LETA KEENS

There are stargazing tours at the Sydney Observatory (*www.sydneyobservatory.com .au; 9921 3485*) nightly at 8.15pm (8.30pm in December and January). They cost $15 for adults.

* * *

THE MOST BEAUTIFUL THING WE CAN EXPERIENCE IS THE MYSTERIOUS. IT IS THE SOURCE OF ALL TRUE ART AND ALL SCIENCE. HE TO WHOM THIS EMOTION IS A STRANGER, WHO CAN NO LONGER PAUSE TO WONDER AND STAND RAPT IN AWE, IS AS GOOD AS DEAD: HIS EYES ARE CLOSED.

Albert Einstein

* * *

By Water

Swimming

Our ocean and harbour pools provide that winning formula of seawater minus the rips and dumpers. They weren't always so popular, though. In Victorian times many locals tried to stop them being built, for fear of encouraging 'undesirables' (otherwise known as 'men swimming naked', a common occurrence in the early days of the colony).

Even at the beginning of last century neck-to-knee costumes were required, bathing was segregated between the sexes, a Sydney archbishop claimed that even watching swimming was immoral, and Randwick Council fined swimmers for wearing costumes in public.

McIvers Baths *(Beach St, Coogee)* perched on a cliff-face between Wylie's Baths (see page 132) and the beach, and built in 1886, is the last remaining women-only seawater pool in Australia. It was granted an exemption from the *Anti-Discrimination Act* in 1995 to keep it that way. The Randwick Ladies Amateur Swimming Club has been running the joint since 1922. Two past devotees of the pool were Fanny Durack and Mina Wylie, who won gold and silver at the 1912 Stockholm Olympics.

On the other side of the harbour is another beauty, the sandy-bottomed **North Narrabeen Rock Pool** *(Peal Place)*, built during the Depression. With its main pool, lap pool and children's wading pool, you could almost call it a swimming complex. Swimming lessons are held here on weekend mornings in summer and winter.

One of the oldest surviving pools in Australia, and with its own beach, is the lovely old timber boardwalked **Dawn Fraser Baths** *(Elkington Park, Balmain)*, named after the Olympic champion who trained here as a kid. The country's first water polo game happened here in the 1880s.

Tour Boats

The most unusual tour from Circular Quay is aboard *Deerubbun*, a WWII torpedo recovery vessel run by **Tribal Warrior** *(www.tribalwarrior .org; 9699 3491)*, a non-profit Aboriginal organisation. You'll be greeted with a traditional welcome dance, find out about the history of Sydney from an Indigenous perspective and maybe even sample a bit of bush tucker along the way. As well as cultural tours, Tribal Warrior operates a training scheme for disadvantaged Indigenous and non-Indigenous young people with the aim of helping them find employment in the maritime industries.

For unique water views, step inside, folks, for a tour of **Tank Stream** – technically a drain. The settlement of Sydney was centred on a stream of fresh water that bubbled up near the town hall and flowed out into the harbour. As the town grew, water needs increased, and Arthur Phillip gave convicts the job of deepening the stream and creating storage tanks for it, hence the name the Tank Stream. Over the years, it was diverted and covered, but it still acts as a stormwater drain for the CBD. Tours happen twice a year through the **Historic Houses Trust** *(www.hht.net.au)*.

Glide By

You may find the intense silence of gliding a little disconcerting at first. But then, as you and your pilot ascend over the Camden Valley – taking in views to the Blue Mountains in one direction, and in the other towards the city in the distance – the peace and quiet up there allows you to tune in to your other senses, as you focus in on the subtle colours of the landscape and watch the clouds changing forms. And, as you realise that you're using the same air currents that birds use to soar, it all starts to seem perfectly natural…and extremely addictive. Visit Southern Cross Gliding Club *(www.gliding.com.au)* at Camden.

Kayaking

Apart from swimming in it or surfing on it, you can't get much closer to the water than in a kayak.

There's something quite mesmerising about the whole sensation of being virtually *in* Middle Harbour – just you, a paddle and a little boat, gliding gracefully along. It's also the perfect way to develop fantastic upper-body strength in next to no time while exploring some of the lesser-known parts of our city.

Starting from the Spit, there are hundreds of bays and points to paddle to. You could drop in to Flat Rock Beach at Garigal National Park. More than 100 species of birds and animals have been spotted in the park recently, including koalas, white-bellied sea eagles and diamond pythons. **Sydney Harbour Kayaks** *(www.sydneyharbourkayaks.com.au)* rents one- and two-person kayaks by the hour. They also run a range of tours, including a Silvertop tour for "those still young at heart but perhaps not so young in years". ∎

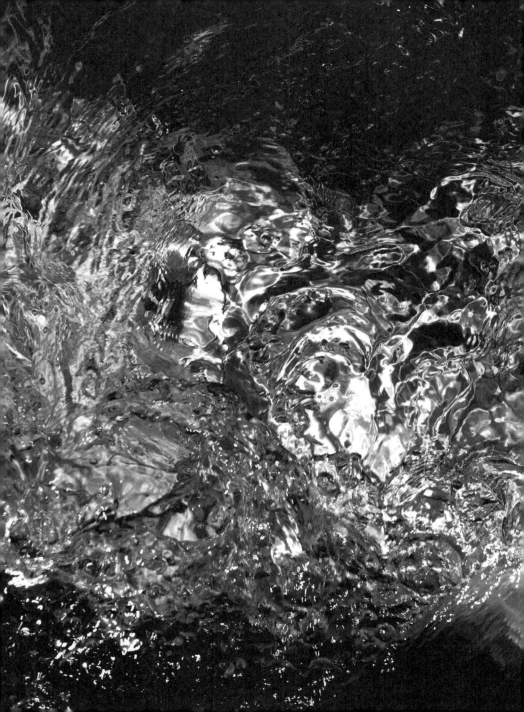

TRAVEL
Places to Reach

-------------------------------- • --------------------------------

I TRAVEL NOT TO GO ANYWHERE, BUT TO GO. I TRAVEL
FOR TRAVEL'S SAKE. THE GREAT AFFAIR IS TO MOVE.

Robert Louis Stevenson

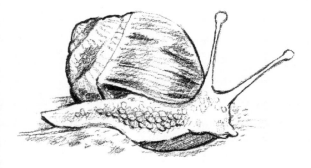

nurture

motion

travel

small

play

gather

Seductive as Sydney is, there also comes a time and a need to escape its charms. Fortunately one of the best things about the city is that it's close to many getaways that can rest the body, expand the mind or tickle the senses. Within a couple of hours or so of the CBD you'll find a cornucopia of delights: from famous surf beaches to mystical bush; coastlines rich with seashells to stylish wineries. The only problem, it seems, is that there are more opportunities for day trips and weekends away than there are weekends to go away. But don't despair. Start now and continue until old age. And remember that every escape from routine is a deliberately slow pursuit. Some, we suggest, are just slower than others.

Time Out

Island Hopping

If holidaying is as much about the journey as the destination, then island hopping in the harbour offers up some of Sydney's greatest adventures and getaways.

Cockatoo Island, at nearly 18 hectares, is the biggest in the harbour and the latest to get a ferry service. It is described as being like "bushwalking in the rust belt", among fabulous industrial equipment that looks like an art installation in this setting. An enormous chimney glimmers like silk in the evening light (apparently caused by ground-up shells in the concrete). Sandstone buildings, to house convicts en route from Norfolk Island, are both beautiful and chilling. This was a brutal place for those convicts sentenced to hard labour, and quarries on the island provided stone for part of Circular Quay.

Shark Island is much more benign than it sounds, named because of its shape rather than the wildlife around it. It's got a lovely rotunda, lots of picnic tables and not very much else. The only way to get there (unless you want to book out the entire island for your private event) is by ferry on the weekend.

Clark Island, another peaceful spot just off Darling Point, can be booked for your exclusive use, or a group of friends can get together, pay $5 each and spend the day there (contact NPWS). You can do some gentle bushwalking or poke around in rockpools before settling down in the shade of a rocky overhang to enjoy the picnic lunch you brought with you.

Fort Denison, close to the Opera House, looks like a prime spot these days, but convicts weren't so convinced. For a while it was used for pretty tough punishment, then for defence, but these days a pleasant brunch and tour of the Martello tower is about the sum of it. The only way to visit Pinchgut, as it's otherwise known, is by a National Parks tour.

• **Ferry timetables** *(www.sydneyferries.info)*
• **Cockatoo Island** *(www.harbourtrust.gov.au) For a full history, maps and tour information.*
• **NPWS** *(www.nationalparks.nsw.gov.au; 9247 5033) Bookings for Clark Island and Port Denison tours.* • **Matilda Cruises** *(www .matilda.com.au) Services to Shark Island.*

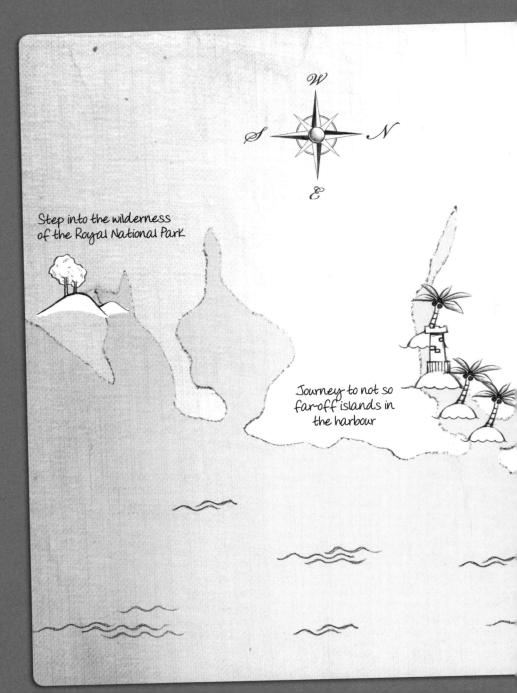

Step into the wilderness
of the Royal National Park

Journey to not so
far-off islands in
the harbour

Blue Mountains, the height of
old-fashioned respite

Grape escapes in
the Hunter Valley

Collect your calm at
the Baha'i Temple

Mystical and magical
Hawkesbury River

The eternally youthful
Umina Beach

Royal National Park

Amid the spectacular coastal wilderness and open woodlands of the Royal National Park is an incredible natural diversity that is packed into a relatively small area less than 40km from the centre of Sydney.

The park was established back in 1879, which makes it the oldest in Australia. And in the world, it's second in years only to Yellowstone in the US. Its majesty makes you wonder if this wasn't the place that inspired the phrase 'the great outdoors'.

The little township of **Bundeena** serves the park, and just heading here has the effect of slowing and calming you down. By car, turn off the Princes Hwy just past Sutherland and you'll be in the park almost right away. Or take a train to Cronulla and catch the prettiest little ferry we've ever seen 20 minutes across Port Hacking.

Our favourite sleepover – although there are plenty to choose from – is **Moonya** (an Aboriginal word for 'safe retreat'), which is available for rental and accommodates up to nine. It's comfortable and welcoming, but not so luxurious that you're going to fret about bringing in a little sand on your feet. With its lovely big balcony looking through trees to the water, courtyards that catch the sun throughout the day and an exceedingly open fireplace for winter, it's the sort of place that could seduce you into doing absolutely nothing at all.

But then, there's too much to explore in the area to sit still for long. If you're tough enough (and not toting a human caravan of under-fives), contemplate a hike to the beautiful **Uloola Falls** where you can camp for one night only.

The track travels past Waterfall Station to **Audley Weir**, a lovely old-fashioned picnic and boating spot where you can easily imagine yourself in Victorian times. On the way you'll see Gymea lilies, waratahs, banksias and woody pears. There's also a spectacular 30km Coast Track (see page 117).

There are more gentle bushwalks to Aboriginal rock carvings beyond Jibbon Beach, and to the remnants of a midden on the spit beyond Bonnie Vale. Nearby is a far more recent archaeological site, the remains of a cluster of holiday shacks that were built from the '20s onwards, but which have been gradually demolished over recent years as their owners have died off. Yes, we know this is National Park land but there's something incredibly poignant about the demise of such simple structures and the ghosts of summers past lingering in the air.

If you have a car, drive into the heart of the park and see masses of Christmas bush and bottlebrush in summer, plus a magical grove of waratah. Listen out for lyrebirds and bower birds, and you might even see the Indonesian rusa deer, which was introduced to the park a century ago. These days, the deers are considered pests but the description doesn't seem to fit.

And if you can't be bothered leaving the comfort of the balcony, don't fret; you can explore next time.

• **NPWS** *(www.nationalparks.nsw.gov.au; 1300 361 967) Lists walks and facilities, and provides further information and maps.*
• *Campers must enquire at the* **Royal National Park Visitor's Centre** *(Farnell Ave, Audley; 9542 0648)* • *See www.south coastholidays.com.au for accommodation, including Moonya.*

Hawkesbury River

A dinghy at the weather-aged jetty of Wondabyne promises a magical journey, if only you'll step inside its dilapidated frame. It's tempting to climb aboard, armed only with a fishing line, a sunhat and a packed lunch. Then, trousers rolled up and water lapping at the little boat, row out onto the cool surface of the historic river – the kookaburras, whip birds and sea eagles heralding a day of peaceful revelry.

Take in the charm of the fibro cottages crouching alongside the river, which is called Deerubbun by the Aborigines. You can visit one of the many fringing national parks, from rainforests and mangroves to drier open woodlands, where rock art preserves the identity of Aboriginal tribes in 200 million-year-old sandstone.

Back in the dinghy again, row out among the pelicans waiting for fish or castoffs from the prawn fishermen trawling behind the mangroves. Call in on one of the locals whose only regular visitor is the Hawkesbury Riverboat postman, who will take you with him for a small fee. Once upon a time, there were many posties delivering mail by river; this is the last one. "I'd say we're looking after between one and two thousand people in about eight or nine communities," says Andrew Davey, whose family bought the mail run (which started in 1910) in 1979. He's the skipper of the *Hawkesbury Explorer*, which these days delivers practically anything that will fit on the ferry – including you, if you want to contemplate the vastness of the mighty river, navigable for more than 100km with 1100km of foreshore fringe.

The English novelist Anthony Trollope spent two days on the river and was so affected by the scenery that he wrote: "The Hawkesbury has neither castles or islands, nor has it bright, clear water like the Rhine, but the headlands are higher, the bluffs are bolder, and the turns and manoeuvres of the course which the waters have made for themselves are grander, and to me more enchanting than those of either the European or the [Mississippi]." Well, locals knew that all along.

Brooklyn Village is set in the Ku-Ring-Gai Chase National Park and is the gateway to the lower Hawkesbury River. It's about a 45-minute scenic drive up the Pacific Hwy, or an hour on one of Australia's most scenic railway journeys, along the northern railway line to the Hawkesbury River Railway Station. If you're flush you can take a seaplane flight from Rose Bay.

From Brooklyn, you can catch a 10-minute ferry to **Dangar Island**. On arrival at the wharf you'll see rows of brightly coloured wheelbarrows, the only means for local residents to transport supplies around the 30-hectare island. Beyond walking, swimming, fishing or paddling, there's nothing to do here. You'll either love or hate Dangar Island; it's bliss for your authors but the height of heebie-jeebie creepiness for Oliver, our normally Zen-like photographer.

• **Hawkesbury River Tourist Information Centre** *(5 Bridge St, Brooklyn; www.hawkesburyriver.org.au; 9985 7064) Information on boat hire, accommodation and tours.* • **Riverboat Post Run** *(Dangar Rd, Brooklyn; 9985 7566) Join the four-hour run from 9.30am Monday to Friday, leaving from the ferry wharf, Brooklyn, at 9.30am (return around lunchtime).* • **Sydney Seaplanes** *(www.seaplanes.com.au; 1300 732 752) Departs Rose Bay.* • **Dangar ferry service** *(9985 7605)*

Baha'i Temple

This is only a short trip from the centre of Sydney, but it's an alternative destination where time seems ever so slightly suspended. Maybe it is the mystical air surrounding the place that makes a visit here seem slow. The 38m-high white, domed Baha'i Temple is so distinctive that pilots often use it for navigation, so you shouldn't have any problem finding it as you wind along Mona Vale Rd.

One of only seven of its kind in the world, the giant temple was built between 1957 and 1961 by Sydney architect John Brogan, whose brief was to create an elegant structure set high in natural bushland and capable of accommodating up to 600 people. The temple has nine sides and nine entrances, which represent the unity of the human race under the one God, irrespective of ethnicity and religious background. This is the foundation of the Baha'i faith, which was established in Iran in the mid-19th century.

White quartz aggregate on the large exterior walls gives the temple an iridescent spiritual shimmer, while the lace curtain windows make it feel almost homely. The lantern on top of the dome was lifted into place by helicopter – the first time this method of construction was used on a major building site in Sydney.

There's a beautifully maintained garden stretching over nine calm and leafy hectares that exude a fitting calm. There's a sign near the temple telling you that all talking must be done outside the building and then, you gather, in respectful tones.

The interior itself is simple, with lots of benches facing the podium and Persian rugs on the floor. Every Sunday at 11am, you can attend a 40-minute service that features readings from the sacred writings of major world religions. But here's the cool part – no sermons or lectures are allowed. As the Baha'i faith has no priesthood, ordinary members of the community read the texts. And there's no collection because only Baha'is are permitted to donate to the temple's upkeep.

• **Baha'i Temple** *(Mona Vale Rd, Ingleside; 9998 9221) Open daily from 9am to 5pm.*

Hunter Valley

The Hunter Valley used to be the kind of place you brought your secretary for a naughty weekend, says winemaker Toby Evans from Evans Wines & Antiques. Nowadays it's a little more on-the-map, not the place you can sneak away to private little B&Bs and dimly lit tasting rooms, but there's still some of the Hunter-of-old among the vineyards if you know where to look.

Pepper Tree's winemaker Chris Cameron reckons the stars are brighter in the Hunter Valley. It's certainly worth pondering while you chat over a drop of sublime merlot or rich, buttery chardonnay. The vineyard is widely known as one of Australia's most awarded – in recent years it has won more than 200 awards and medals nationally and internationally.

Stop in at **Tulloch Wines** too, which began in 1895 when John Younie Tulloch accepted the 43-acre property as settlement of a debt. Watch out for the vintage delivery truck, which still runs, parked outside.

Talk antiques to Toby Evans at **Evans Wines & Antiques**, which was established by his father, the late Len Evans. Like a small

number of Australian producers, Toby grows gamay, a purple-coloured grape variety used to make red wines like the deliciously light-bodied and fruity beaujolais. It is a very old cultivar, dating back to the 15th century. The Evans vineyard is also known for its Howard Shiraz, a classic, soft and elegant red.

On your way home through Cessnock, a provincial town that seems permanently stuck in the 50s, stop into the **Marthaville Craft & Gift Centre** for glassware, cards, linen and clothing all made by local artists. The centre is situated in Cessnock's oldest sawn timber home. It was built by builder, saw miller, civil magistrate, district coroner and shire councillor George Brown in 1855. Under the galvanised roof, timber shingles can still be seen under the edge of the eaves. Three of the rooms have retained their original fireplaces and cedar mantelpieces.

• **Hunter Valley Wine Country Visitor Information Centre** *(www.winecountry.com.au; 4990 0900)* • **Pepper Tree Wines** *(Halls Rd, Pokolbin; www.peppertreewines.com.au)* • **Tulloch Wines** *(cnr DeBeyers and McDonalds Rds, Pokolbin; www.tulloch.com.au)* • **Evans Family Wines & Antiques** *(92 Broke Rd, Pokolbin)* • **Marthaville Craft & Gift Centre** *(200 Wollombi Rd, Cessnock; 4991 4634)*

Umina Beach

Umina Beach is a mere 90 minutes up the F3 from Sydney. It's not flash but is *real* in a way coastal towns used to be. Real in a way even Sydney might have been before it gave way to the push-and-shove of international commerce and the pursuit of the dollar instead of the wave. The name is said to mean 'repose', so this place can't be bad.

On the shores of Broken Bay, it sits at the convergence of the major waterways of Pittwater, the Hawkesbury River and Brisbane Waters. Perhaps because of this aquatic juxtaposition, the daily rituals themselves are infused with the feel, taste or idea of water: the morning surf, the pit stop for a chicken curry pie from Ron at the widely awarded **Bremen's Pattisserie** *(West St)*, or for fresh barramundi from outside the Ocean Beach Hotel (OBH) and perhaps stopping for a cooling ale in the pub while you're there.

Established as a resort town in 1917, Umina (or 'Um and Ah' as it's affectionately known) is laid-back with a capital 'L'. (Except maybe for Friday nights when it seems like every youngster in the town hangs out in the front bar of the OBH and the older residents at the local club, the Umina Bowlo.)

The ocean beach is taken over by a cheerful menagerie of surfers, parents with kids, holidaymakers from the local caravan park and dog owners taking their charges for a game of tussle. Join them with your board, esky and sunhat.

When you tire of relaxing on the gritty, beige-coloured shore or staring out into the distance at Lion Island and ritzy Palm Beach, a ferry ride away, head to the nearby **Brisbane Waters National Park**. It holds 12,000 hectares of spectacular rugged sandstone country including Aboriginal engravings, bushwalking tracks, wildflowers and wildlife, providing plenty of challenges for the more active holidaymaker.

• **NPWS** *(www.nationalparks.nsw.gov.au) Walks on the Central Coast, including Brisbane Waters.* • *For more information about the Central Coast (including Umina, Ettalong and the Entrance) visit www.visitcentralcoast.com.au.*

A Journey of the Mind

Hundreds of books offer portholes into different Sydney perspectives, including: *Seven Poor Men of Sydney* by Christina Stead; *Camille's Bread* by Amanda Lohrey; *Lillian's Story* by Kate Grenville; *Ride On Stranger* by Kylie Tennant; *Bobbin Up* by Dorothy Hewett; *Manly Girls* by Elisabeth Wynhausen; *Candy* by Luke Davies; *Oscar and Lucinda* by Peter Carey; *The Harp in the South* by Ruth Park; *Aunts up the Cross* by Robin Dalton; Cliff Hardy novels by Peter Corris; and *The Cross* by Mandy Sayer.

The Blue Mountains area is a spectacular World Heritage wilderness. It's also the kind of place your old nanna or rich uncle would take you for high tea at one of the old-fashioned cafes, or to browse a collection of antiques in one of the charming stores.

Perhaps because of the weather, which can be rather nippy and, well, mountainish, the place has an almost olde English feel about it. Certainly the pace isn't going to wear you out, which is why, increasingly, this area is home to those who work in Sydney but want to commute to somewhere more tranquil after the clock turns to 5pm.

Of course the Blue Mountains also attracts stressed-out city dwellers looking for a place to lose themselves for hours, or days, by stopping off for a few spectacular views and **bushwalks** at places like Echo Point, Katoomba and Wentworth Falls; or by visiting interesting historical attractions and browsing in the many charming galleries and antique shops while strolling around villages such as Leura. The local population is cosmopolitan and creative, with this area attracting far more than its fair share of artists, composers and writers.

One well known past denizen is artist **Norman Lindsay**, whose home includes one of the most-visited National Trust gardens in Australia. 'Springwood' was built in the mid-1890s for the Sydney department store owner Francis Foy. Norman Lindsay and his (soon to be) second wife Rose Soady bought the property in 1912 and re-named the estate.

Today, you can feel Lindsay's spirit. The cottage is presented as the showplace of a major collection of his work including watercolours, sculptures, ship models, novels and an exhibition of models from his classic children's book *The Magic Pudding*. The beautiful garden includes outdoor swimming and bathing pools, established rose-covered pergolas and sculptures, fountains and urns, and there's a hint of fairies or at least imps around every turn.

If you feel like a little more greenery as balm to the soul, there's no better place than **Mount Tomah Botanic Garden**. When the fog rises from this 28-hectare garden, the views over the mountains are breathtaking – it probably helps that, in the foreground, there's the most amazing array of plants and trees (more than 5000 different species, at last count) in a sensitively landscaped setting.

The grouping of plants is pretty unusual – all done geographically, so you can go on a bit of a whirlwind world tour in just a few hours, checking out rhododendrons from the Himalayas, proteas from South Africa, with a wander through the southern beeches of Australia while you're at it.

'Tomah' is thought to be the local Aboriginal word for 'tree fern', one of the main natives of the area, along with eucalypts. George Caley, a plant collector, was the first white man to come across the area, in 1804, and originally called it Fern Tree Hill.

• **Mount Tomah Botanic Garden** *(Bells Line of Road, via Bilpin; www.rbgsyd.nsw.gov.au)*
• *For information about accommodation and activities, go to www.visitbluemountains. com.au.* • **Norman Lindsay Gallery and Museum** *(14 Norman Lindsay Crescent, Faulconbridge; www.normanlindsay.com.au)* •
(Opposite) **Glastonbell** *(Chiefly Rd, Bell; 6355 2616; www.glastonbell.com.au) At the very top of the Blue Mountains near Mt Victoria.* ∎

Blue Mountains Break

Essay

Heading towards Glastonbell in the Blue Mountains, the name of my destination conjures images of crusaders and female Dakinis, of heroic deeds and intrigues. Winding up the road past quaint mountain houses, a small bush track discreetly branches off and meanders among gnarled gums and banksias. And there, straddling a high ridge, sits Glastonbell, 410 acres of natural beauty that offers a respite for those wishing to delve into the mysteries of life, nature and Aboriginal law. Enter here for a holiday with a difference, offering friendship, regeneration and empowerment.

The weekend custodian greets us with tea and laughter. The shared kitchen and lounge of a homely country house provides a pivot point for learning about the founders of Glastonbell, Aboriginal heritage and the ancestral spirit of the sanctuary. This is a 'dreaming place' where contact with other spirits is possible for those who can tune in and where the connection to the earth is emphasised to all who stay.

The budget accommodation is eco-friendly and informal, comprising the main house, the lodge for larger groups, three cabins and several tent sites.

I choose the 'Cube', a little cubby hut on the ridge's edge overlooking the world. I lie in bed watching the revolving heavens, listening to the rustle of small nocturnal animals. The first light of dawn nudges me awake and I follow sandy paths to Sunset Rock, past sandstone outcrops carved by the wind, rain and sun. Below, the mist swirls and plays in the gorges, while the rising sun's gentle brilliance weaves intricate patterns of light and shade across craggy surfaces.

After meditation, we share breakfast of porridge, jam and soft talk. I wander back to my 3m x 4m palace, have an open-air shower behind a corrugated-iron screen and join new friends to explore evocatively named walking trails. Countless sacred and ceremonial Indigenous sites are found among the mountains and valleys that surround Glastonbell.

We descend to the valley floor along walls of stone and yawning cave mouths where trees hold fast to the walls tangling themselves into life. We walk quietly, a tinkle of laughter or a sigh of awe rising from our little group. Trickling water splashes over a rock ledge cooling us on our way down to where corridors of stone lead to caves like ballrooms, furnished with ancient benches and dappled with green light. We ascend a narrow opening to a 'cathedral' carved from rock, an altar of stone and a majestic view over the deep valley.

Glastonbell (details opposite) is a unique alternative to the hedonistic pleasures of usual holiday options, and focuses on peaceful reflection. At the end of my visit, I feel renewed and inspired, as if I had taken in more than just mountain air.

GLENDA MORGAN

Slow-mo ⟹

Holiday at Home

Picture your life in Sydney over the last week, imagining the ground you've covered shaded on a map. Like most of us, you probably took the same routes to the same places on the same days by the same means. Perhaps during your undeviating week you imagined a holiday – after you've cleared this busy period or that frigging debt. But why not take a holiday right now? Block out 'slow days' on your calendar, and keep them free. Seize the mood and negotiate yourself a 'mental-health day' from work. Embrace Sydney as if for the first time, actually sample some of the things about which tourists rave, forget what you know and focus on experiencing something new.

- Detour. Turn off the main road and explore a new suburb; get off the train or bus a few stops before yours and walk the rest of the way home. Walk a completely different way to work.

- Catch a ferry, any ferry.

- Travel to the other side of the city and dine at an ethnic restaurant or shop for foods you've never eaten before.

- Head to a bar and sample unfamiliar beers or wines from the smallest producers.

- Join a tour group (or tag along close enough to listen for free, until you're chased off).

- Have high tea at one of the city's hotels: nibbling on salmon sandwiches and petit four and sipping Earl Grey tea with raised pinky.

- Offer to housesit for a friend while they go away (or swap places with them for a weekend). Ask them to leave a list of their favourite things to do in the neighbourhood, and try out as many of their suggestions as you can.

SMALL
Slow Things for Fast Kids

- • -

66 THE MOST EFFECTIVE KIND OF EDUCATION IS THAT
A CHILD SHOULD PLAY AMONGST LOVELY THINGS. 99

Plato

nurture

motion

travel

small

play

gather

'Slow' and 'kids' is not an oxymoron. But there's a trick to it: keep things simple. Whether at home or out and about, children are a terrific excuse to play and be frivolous.

Make your own fun at home: erect a tent, zip yourselves in and tell ghost stories by torchlight. Make bread from scratch. Plant herbs in a terracotta pot and start a nature table for found objects like a bird's nest, autumn leaf or cicada casings. Life cycles have a wonderful way of putting things into perspective.

Thinking of heading out? Sydney has a habit of confounding you with choice. Beach or bush? Museum or playground? Go for whatever suits your mood, nurture body and soul, foster the imagination or learn a thing or two about a thing or two. Feel your pulse soften and your heart open up to life in the slow lane.

Playgrounds

Sydney's parks and playgrounds are little pieces of heaven – organic places to refuel on fresh air. And it's free entertainment for your children while you sprawl beneath a lemony eucalypt and the day's newspaper.

Most playgrounds nowadays are dazzlingly innovative, taking advantage of bushy or harbour postcodes and themed to tug imaginations. Run-of-the-mill monkey bars and old swings have been replaced with tummy-tickling flying foxes, fabulous climbing frames and wobbly bridges. Such natural elements as rock sculptures, grassy borders and wooden ramps to this and that sit alongside clever inventions – noise boxes, sand that stays damp for superior sandcastles and pumps for summer water play.

Seasonal and Scenic

Some playgrounds are either seasonal or are defined by their location. In winter, for instance, the **Camperdown Memorial Rest Park Playground** (*between Australia and Lennox Sts, Newtown*) is gritty and fun but lacks shade. Others are drenched in trees, and are ideal in summer. We adore **Beauchamp Park** (*cnr Nicholson and Darling Sts, Chatswood*).

Well-positioned others include the harbour-hugging **Lyne Park** (*New South Head Rd, Rose Bay*), while **Elkington Park** (*White St, Balmain*) overlooks the water and has plenty of shade. **Apex Park** (*Surfview Rd, Mona Vale*) and **Collaroy Beach** (*Birdwood Ave, Collaroy Beach*) are among the best.

Bush-cushioned

Playgrounds that are surrounded by bushland with walking tracks are perfect for nature-loving families. Our favourites include **Bobbin Head Playground** (*Ku-ring-gai Chase National Park, Bobbin Head Rd, Bobbin Head*), **Steamroller Park** (*Oatley Park Ave, Oatley*) and the **Green Reserve** (*Merriman St, Kyle Bay*).

St Ives Showground (*Mona Vale Rd, St Ives*) has three separate play areas; sporadic gymkanas add to the rural appeal. **Berry Island Reserve** (*Shirley Rd, Wollstonecraft*) offers excellent wooden climbing equipment and a track dotted with plaques with information about Aboriginal heritage.

Tweens and Themes

With its large forts, endless slides, suspension bridges and tyre walks, **Holroyd Gardens Park** *(Walpole St, Merrylands)* is good for older children. So, too, is **Rouse Hill Regional Park** *(Worcester Rd, Rouse Hill)*. Take the bikes and head to the **Road Safety Training Track** *(Walpole St, Merrylands)*; it has a road layout with roundabouts, road signs, pedestrian crossings and road humps. Some parks cleverly combine play areas and cycling tracks: **Bicentennial Park** *(Australia Ave, Homebush Bay)*, for instance, has two large playgrounds as well as extensive bike tracks and a maze. There's also **Ku-ring-gai Bicentennial Park** in West Pymble *(Lofberg St)*.

Train-driver wannabes will adore **Bales Park** *(Stanley St, Chatswood)*, although it's rather small, as well as **Wahroonga Park** *(Coonabarra Rd, Wahroonga)* and the **EG Waterhouse Camellia Gardens** *(President Ave, Caringbah)* – it also has a wonderful garden.

Potential pirates will have to be dragged kicking and screaming from **Little Manly Point** *(Stuart St, Manly)* with its ship theme created from redeveloped old gasworks. **Bicentennial Park** *(Chapman Rd, Glebe)* is a fabulous park for me-hearties with a swinging hammock and a roller slide. There's a boat at **Echo Point Park** *(Babbage Rd, Roseville Chase)*. **Gough Whitlam Park** *(Bayview Ave, Undercliff)* was designed specifically for kids with disabilities – plenty of wheelchair-friendly paths and raised sensory garden beds for touching.

With Animals

The extensive **Central Gardens** *(cnr Betts and Merrylands Rds, Merrylands West)* is bookended by two marvellous playgrounds and has an animal enclosure and aviary. **Lane Cove National Park** *(Lady Game Drive, Chatswood)* contains the Kukundi Wildlife Shelter where you can see native animals recuperating before being released into the wild. **Fairfield City Farm** *(31 Darling St, Abbotsbury; 9823 3222)*, one hour west of Sydney, is a piece of rural paradise. Feed the nursery animals, watch a chick hatch from an egg and learn how to milk a cow in the morning. After lunch (BYO sausages for the barbecue) take in the sheep-shearing and working-dog shows. While you're in the area, visit **Fairfield City Museum** *(cnr Horsley Drive and Oxford St, Smithfield; 9609 3993)*. A village from 1880s is set up with free art and craft every Saturday and in school holidays.

The carefully restored Nutcote *(5 Wallaringa Ave, Neutral Bay; 9953 4453)*, the 1925 home of May Gibbs, is more for nostalgic parents who will enjoy the tour by volunteers – but there are pictures of Bib and Bub, and videos for kids to watch. The pretty English gardens hide such wonderful creatures as a caterpillar hedge, wisteria hysteria and agapanthas panthers. The native garden, including a 150-year-old she-oak, overlooks the water. Children's parties take place on a shady verandah: charming and restorative.

Clever

Some playgrounds warrant a visit simply because of their interesting features. Foe example, there's a huge chessboard at **Burwood Park** (*Park Ave, Burwood*) and the north end of **Hyde Park** (*Elizabeth St*), while **Maluga Passive Park** (*Woods Rd, Sefton*) has a noughts-and-crosses game. A human sundial at **Pimelea Playspace** (*cnr Cowpasture Rd and Horsley Drive, Horsley Park*) offers children an alternative to wristwatches: stand on a spot marked by the month, face an arc of numbers up to 12, and your shadow falls on the correct time.

Mt Annan Botanic Gardens (*Mt Annan Drive, Mt Annan*) is a native garden and the largest botanic garden in Australia; it's made doubly good by the Flannel Flower Maze, negotiated by answering questions on Federation. **Warners Park** (*the Outpost, off Kameruka Rd, Northbridge*) has mirrors that hilariously distort your image. **Brereton Park** (*Bronhill Ave, East Ryde*) has a grassy hill marvellous for go-kart racing (BYO go-kart or cardboard sled).

St Leonards Park (*Miller St, North Sydney*) has some wonderful musical instruments. Play with perspective and have a cup of green tea at the **Chinese Garden of Friendship** (*Pier St, cnr Harbour St, Darling Harbour; 9281 6863*). While very small, the traditional Chinese design (using miniature trees and paths that turn on themselves) makes this garden feel much larger.

Putney Park Playground (*Pellisier Rd, Putney*) has, amid the rope climbing frames and possibly the longest slide in Sydney, two landscaped paddling pools that are linked by a creek.

Look for tactile and colourful art among the climbing equipment at **Hallstrom Reserve Playspace** (*Small St, Willoughby*) – noise boxes are another drawcard here – and **Passmore Reserve** (*Campbell Pde, Manly Vale*). You might see carvings of people in trees, sculptures of animals, reclining figures and mural walls.

Slow-mo ⇒

Backyard Wonders

After a week of school, swimming lessons, soccer training, piano practice, homework and getting in and out of a car there's nothing quite like rushing into the backyard and staying put.

- Turn your tent into a yurt by filling it with as many scatter cushions as you can find.

- Flop onto the trampoline and count the evening stars as they blink awake. Look for the Southern Cross.

- Talk dad into frying thin sausages on the portable gas ring and eat them with a fork, the grease running down your wrists and into the lawn.

- Collect cicada casings. Borrow a book about them from the local library and draw a picture to sit beside the display of casings.

- Lie on the lawn and mingle with the scent of port wine magnolia and freshly mown grass.

Thrills and Spills

We'll talk about Luna Park *(Olympic Park, Milsons Point; 9922 6644)* a lot before we actually go. Should we start with a biggie: the Rotor, say, and work our way down to the Laughing Clowns? Or start with the Ferris wheel – for good views – and work up the courage to the Ranger. We'll usually warm up inside Coney Island – most activities are originals from the 1930s. It's cool. We can stay there for an hour, maybe two. The slides in there are pretty exciting, but the big one takes us ages to work up to – we look at it a lot first. We always go on the Dodgems. Mum says we're a real menace on them, but it's no fun unless you bump into everybody at least once. The Wild Mouse is good, too, but my dad says it doesn't compare to the Big Dipper, the rollercoaster that was removed in 2001 because locals complained about the screams.

Sometimes during summer an ice rink is set up under the big top and we've also seen divers climb a long, long ladder and plunge into a tiny pool. Unreal. We always take time out to walk along the boardwalk. You can see, in the garden beds, mini bronze sculptures by local artist, Peter Kingston, of stuff like a ferry and Luna Park's laughing face. He also draws pictures of endangered animals in chalk on the pathway – messages to Prime Minister John Howard, who sometimes walks around the shores, too.

JOSH, AGED NEARLY 9
(WITH HELP FROM MUM)

Life Lessons

Chef's Hat: During the holidays children as young as seven don aprons and stand along stainless-steel benches to learn the skills necessary to prepare a three-course meal. Humour is an essential ingredient at **Accoutrement** (*611 Military Rd, Mosman; 9969 4911*), and participants are encouraged to get their hands sticky and floury. The art of baking, decorating and (best fun of all) consuming cup cakes is the specialty in the commercial-grade kitchens at **Rowie's Cakes** (*78 Livingstone Rd, Marrickville; 9950 0346*).

Geeks and Freaks: The **CSIRO education department** (*www.csiro.au/sydcsirosec; 9490 8677*) holds science workshops in 10 Sydney locations every school holidays. They are well organised and aimed at entertaining as well as educating children. **Fizzics Education** (*5 St James Place, Seven Hills; 9674 2191*) is a mobile science experiment group who visit playgroups, birthdays and families, while **Professor Plums** (*Shop 1, Ernest Place, Crows Nest; 9906 7441*) is the place for chess tournaments and science camps.

Surf and Turf: Every weekend at various times, **Manly Surf School** (*North Steyne Rd, Manly; 9977 6977*) teaches grommets from age five the basics of standing on a board, surf safety and etiquette. The school provides boards and wetsuits for the lessons and the instructors are surfers with first-aid skills. Other schools are also at Long Reef, Collaroy and Palm Beach; ring the Manly school for all bookings.

Flash Dance: During school holidays, kids can shake their bootie at one of the workshops put on by the **Sydney Dance Company** (*the Wharf, Pier 4, Hickson Rd, Walsh Bay; 9258 4818*). Held in the studios used by the dancers, they cover funk, hip hop and jazz (among others), and are taught by professional dancers and choreographers.

Acting Out: Drama queens will fit right in to one of the excellent courses from the prestigious drama school **NIDA** (*215 Anzac Pde, Kensington; 9697 7620*). They teach voice projection, singing and dancing as well as acting, all of it in front of a camera. Running away to the circus becomes a possibility after a three-day workshop at **Circus Unique** (*St Scholastica's College, 4 Avenue Rd, Glebe; 9810 6090*). Learn how to juggle, do tricks on the trapeze, walk on stilts and generally be acrobatic. The workshop culminates in a mini circus performance.

Must-Have Memberships

The fabulous **Stanton Library** (*234 Miller St, North Sydney; 9936 8400*) devotes an entire level (downstairs) to a marvellous collection of children's books. There is story time, toys to play with, artwork by local school children to examine and a comic book section to peruse. There's also quiet areas, TV stations and computer tables, as well as a community park at the rear of the building.

Zoofriends of **Taronga Zoo** (*Bradleys Head Rd, Mosman; www.zoofriends.org.au 9968 2822*) enter for free – only two visits and it's paid off – making it perfectly acceptable for an amble after school. Zoofriends are able to tour the zoo after hours in a series called Behind the Scenes where you'll learn how the exhibits are fed, trained and protected. Along with its sloping gardens, weaving paths, spaciously renovated enclosures and expansive views of the harbour, the Backyard to Bush exhibit features a full-size environmentally friendly house and backyard.

Our spirits always lift inside the **Powerhouse Museum** (*500 Harris St, Ultimo; 9217 0111*). It is partly because of the vast range of exhibits, which are always relevant and interesting. But also due to the high number of staff encouraging kids to roam, touch, listen and learn. The members' lounge is well stocked with magazines, drinks, biscuits and toys. Bliss.

The Kids' Club is for members of the **Art Gallery of New South Wales** (*Art Gallery Rd, the Domain; 9225 1744*), though Art Zone for teenagers is open to non-members. It's becoming bigger and more popular every year because of its knack of catapulting children into the wonderful world of art, colour and composition in a way that no crayons-and-paper babysitting activity can. Look at the current exhibition while there, too.

Wildlife Wonders

At dusk, the bush around Sydney throbs with Tawny frogmouth owls, fruit bats and possums. Grab a torch and join guided bush walks organised by local councils. Or visit your local park and stand very still; let your eyes adjust and look up. Pure magic.

Ku-ring-gai Wildflower Garden's (*420 Mona Vale Rd, St Ives; 9440 8552*) Senses Track encourages a sensory tour of the bush, crushing leaves and listening to birds. There are heaps of fun things to do during the Wildflower festival in August.

The Coastal Environment Centre (*Lake Park Rd, North Narrabeen; 9970 6905*) has weekend holiday activities like spotlighting, guided rock platform walks, and looking through microscopes at the tiny creatures found in rockpools. Afterwards, take your new rockpool skills to the beach; one of the best is the northern end of Balmoral Beach.

Out and About

The **Swain Gardens** (*77 Stanhope Rd, Killara*) is a heavenly blend of formal garden beds and lawns framed by low stone terraces and circular paths, bequeathed to the National Trust in the 1970s by Mr Mick Swain. Sydney girls are very grateful, too, because it's the sort of fairy dell in which they can really let down their golden tresses, assume the airs and graces of a queen or host a fairy party beneath the gazebo. Beware of the goblins living in the dark bamboo forest on the edge of the garden and, of course, pesky schoolboys.

The **Australian National Maritime Museum** (*2 Murray St, Darling Harbour; 9298 3777*) is a wonderful place for kids who yearn to be pirates and sailors. Here, they'll see that submarine life on board HMAS *Onslow* in the 60s was cramped and stifling yet fascinating. This boat, designed to be silent and secret so as to spy on the Soviet Union during the cold war, was only decommissioned in 1999. HMAS *Vampire* (launched in 1956) is another excellent exhibit, exactly as it was when the last crew stepped off – uniforms hanging in lockers, photographs of family and orders stuck on to walls.

Head north or south for an hour to a **pick-your-own** farm. Imagine their surprise when they discover that plums and oranges are twisted from the branch of a tree, not put into a supermarket trolley. The season for apples, peaches, plums and pears is December to April. **Montrose Berry Farm** (*Ormond St, Sutton Forest; 4868 1544*), **Cuttaway Creek Raspberry Farm** (*Old Hume Hwy, Mittagong; 4871 1201*) and **Pinecrest Orchard** (*2549 Bells Line of Road, Bilpin; 4567 1143*) all open their gates for public picking.

Watch dancers from the **Australian Ballet** (*www.australianballet.com.au; 9250 7777*) train, followed by coaching, a rehearsal and, finally, a fully staged excerpt from a show. ∎

Dreaming about the Dreaming

As far as children are concerned, those hard-boiled eggs you packed are witchety grubs, and as soon as they pick up a pointy stick they're imbued with the spirit of the Guringai people. Such is the atmosphere of West Sydney's Ku-ring-gai Chase National Park, which has 16 walking tracks (ranging from 1km to 4.5km).

The steep decent from the top of a cliff overlooking Pittwater and Palm Beach to the private and breathtaking West Head Beach (*West Head Rd, McCarrs Creek*) is an extraordinary experience. In early winter, the heath banksia is in bloom and attracts hundreds of honeyeaters. You might also hear the noisy Lyrebird's love call during mating season (from May to July).

> ## ONE GENERATION PLANTS THE TREES;
> ## ANOTHER GETS THE SHADE.
>
> Chinese proverb

PLAY
For Sydney's Amusement

- • -

" OUR MINDS NEED RELAXATION, AND GIVE WAY
UNLESS WE MIX WORK WITH A LITTLE PLAY. "

Molière

nurture

motion

travel

small

play

gather

There are so many expectations on the way we behave: as a worker, a parent, friend, partner and citizen. Each role is a box with a set of rules on how we ought to do things. Having responsibilities is all well and good – even welcomed sometimes – but it's equally important to forget how, and even *if*, we're behaving now and then, and just do fun things for the hell of it.

Sydney's unique position gives us a magnificent playground, and plenty of opportunities to find inspiration, be enthralled or just wrap ourselves up in giddy delight. Playing can be personal or shared, stimulating or frivolous, energetic or downright relaxing. From avoiding the cracks in Pitt St to bouncing up and down with 44,000 significant others at the SCG, Sydney's a glorious place to play and you just have to join in.

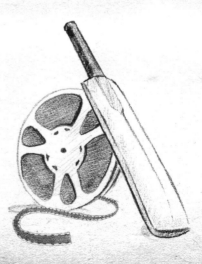

A Year of Play

January in Sydney is about sitting back and letting others do the work. So it's perfect timing for the Sydney Festival (www.sydneyfestival.org.au) and its mix of highbrow, lowbrow and just plain weird entertainment that's often staged in otherwise-overlooked parts of the city.

The OpenAir Cinema (www.stgeorgeopenair.com.au) at Mrs Macquarie's Point allows you to look out over the Harbour Bridge and Opera House, one of the world's most gorgeous backdrops. The Domain also becomes a focal point, as the setting for three of Sydney's favourite musical events: Jazz, Symphony and Opera in the Domain (www.rbgsyd.nsw .gov.au). There's no need to dress up but if you feel like putting on a tiara, no one will bat an eyelid. Bring a picnic and a blanket and, as the sun goes down and the flying foxes make their nightly pilgrimage, listen to some of the most exhilarating music ever written.

Chinese New Year falls between late January and late February, a time for fire crackers and giving gifts or red envelopes containing money or chocolate coins.

It's back to the Domain in **February** for Tropfest (www.tropinc.com), the biggest short-film festival in the world. It has come a long way since film-maker and actor John Polson screened his short film at Darlinghurst's Tropicana Café in the early 90s. Around 200 people turned up to the original, encouraging Polson to start a festival. In the early days, chairs were set up for the audience on Victoria St, but the burgeoning event was eventually moved to the Domain.

Ponder what the developed environment says about Sydney in **March** with the annual National Trust Heritage Festival (www.nsw .nationaltrust.org.au). It has been going for almost 30 years, from the time we realised our city had a heritage worth celebrating and saving. There are always plenty of free exhibitions, walks and workshops, which might range from photos of a Kings Cross diner to a look at the history of the Wentworth Park dog track.

As autumn presents itself in **April**, fiddlers and folksingers come out for the St Albans Festival (www.snalbans.iwarp.com) in the original pioneer town of St Albans. Locals know it as 'the Forgotten Valley' because it has been bypassed by all major road and rail routes out of Sydney.

The city is transformed into a centre of intellectualism and ideas in **May** with the Sydney Writers' Festival (www.swf.org.au), one of the largest of its kind in the world. It embraces all forms of writing from the esoteric to the blockbuster. The most stimulating events are often the most unexpected: perhaps a Chinese author you've never heard of talking about her life or an equally obscure Scottish poet reading his work in a pub.

June is the best time to be left in the dark...for the Sydney Film Festival (www.sydneyfilmfestival.org) and the myriad escape routes it provides into different worlds and cultures. The central venue is the lavish Henry Eli White–designed State Theatre, which is dripping with cast plaster figurines and foliage motifs, and was dubbed 'The Empire's greatest theatre' when it opened in the 20s.

The art world converges on Sydney every couple of years round about **July** for the Sydney Biennale (www.biennaleofsydney.com.au), an exposition of contemporary art. It features a different curator each biennale, so every one has its own flavour. In recent years, we've seen art in disused warehouses, outlying parts of the city and islands in the harbour, and quite often the venue has outshone the artwork. But that's all part of the programme, because what would a celebration of contemporary art be without some heated discussion and plenty of head scratching?

After so much indoor, passive play, raise your aerobic levels in **August** with the City to Surf. It feels like Pitt St at peak hour when you line up with the 59,999 others at College St for the 14km run to Bondi Beach, but Heartbreak Hill in the eastern suburbs soon sorts out the powerhouses from the laggers, and the serious from the Elvis and Humphrey B Bear look-alikes.

September is a breeze, just the way you want it for Bondi's Festival of the Winds (www.aks.org.au). Kite-makers and flyers from all over the world set their creations aloft, filling the skies with colour and movement. If you don't own a kite, don't worry – stalls sell them and there are workshops where you can learn how to make your own. And, as with so many other Sydney events, there are multicultural food stalls, comedy acts, jugglers and loads of other entertainment.

The cliff walk from Bondi to Bronte takes on a surreal edge towards the end of **October** with Sculpture by the Sea (www.sculpturebythesea.com), which has been going since 1997 and is a brilliant way to combine culture with a bit of exercise and a sense of community. There's often a whimsical element to the exhibits, as they play hide-and-seek, turning up in unexpected spots along the coastline.

For sticky beaks – that includes just about everyone, right? – Sydney Open is completely irresistible. It usually takes place one day in **November**, when doors are opened to dozens of buildings that are normally off limits. Apartments, jails, fire stations, banks, power stations, the Masonic Centre, the Royal College of Physicians – you name it, they've all been part of Sydney Open, which is run by the Historic Houses Trust (www.hht.net.au).

Music characterises **December**. But for something other than the usual carol singers and Handel's 'Messiah', the Pinchgut Opera (www.pinchgutopera.com.au) stages rarely performed baroque operas at City Recital Hall, Angel Place. Some may not be related to the season of goodwill (gigantic sea monsters, fathers killing off children – you know, the usual operatic cheer), but there's something very festive about supporting a small, local company that's doing brilliant work, encouraging up-and-coming young talent and throwing some big names into the mix as well.

Essay →

Orienteering

It's been described as 'running while playing chess', which is a pretty daunting prospect when you're hopeless at both. But a quick call to the Orienteering Association of NSW *(www.nsw.orienteering.asn.au)* allayed my fears. You don't need any special gear, beyond non-slip shoes and a rain jacket in winter months, most orienteering events only take a couple of hours, and, unless you choose to live on the edge, there's very little chance of getting lost.

About 40 of us show up to a patch of bushland at Bass Hill in the western suburbs. There are two courses and I opt for the 2.35km beginners' version. I'm bitterly disappointed to be told that, at my chosen level, I won't be requiring a compass. Instead, I'm handed a map, a list of features to navigate by and a card that gets punched with a different pattern at every marker.

We're sent off at two-minute intervals, and the idea is to get around the course as quickly and accurately as possible (rules by which I don't play, of course). I see the more experienced battling through blackberry bushes, but I stick to the tracks, don't get lost, and manage to find every marker. I complete the course in just over 49 minutes without even breaking into a trot.

When I realise an eight-year-old boy has beaten me by several minutes, I decide it's time to go home, doubting whether or not my new orienteering friends are ready to celebrate the virtues of slow and to declare that, by coming last, I am in fact the winner.

LETA KEENS

Slow Sports

Sport is part of Sydney's personality and provides a sense of Australianess. Thankfully, it's not all about being the fastest, strongest or the fittest...

Cricket

When it comes to slow, cricket is the clear winner, and there are few things as nostalgic or comforting as the thwack of leather on willow or the laconic (and occasionally hyperbolic) radio commentary. They are much part of Sydney summer as the scent of frangipani and waiting for a southerly bluster. Compared with most sports – that are intense, confrontational and over in little more than an hour – there's something wonderfully anachronistic about a game that can take five days to play, and where the players actually look like they're having fun.

As spectators at a Test match at the SCG, it's perfectly acceptable to take a good book and to have a natter with friends, or to go off and have a drink – it can be a long time between balls. And you've got to love a sport that, no matter what or where – at the cricket ground or in every second suburban backyard, at an exciting moment or in the middle of a dull patch – unfailingly stops for tea.

AFL

The Sydney Swans are the slowest team in the AFL, not because of their much-maligned short-chipping style (which we won't hear a word against), but because they are led by Buddhist warrior and co-captain Brett Kirk and use the power of meditation to help them focus. The coach's wife teaches meditation, which is no doubt one of the reasons they've been so successful in recent years, winning a flag (oh, see Leo leap!) in 2005.

Lawn Bowls

No game has so successfully reinvented itself as lawn bowls has in recent years. It used to be in nanna territory – an unquestionably slow but supposedly dull sport, further hampered by the particularly daggy uniforms worn by players. And, like many players, the sport was on its last legs until a new generation discovered what the oldies knew all along – lawn bowls is exciting (in its own quiet way), skilful, sociable and a very relaxing way to spend a few hours outdoors.

It helps that the whites have been ditched, and a number of clubs, including **Gladesville Sporties** (cnr Ryde Rd and Swan St; 9816 1773) and **Bondi Bowling Club** (Warners Ave, North Bondi; 9130 2383), now offer barefoot bowls sessions, which cost around $15 per person. Other clubs include: **Alexandria Erskineville Bowling Club** (1 Fox Ave; 9557 5749), **Manly Bowling Club** (Raglan St; 9977 3114), **Ryde City Bowling Club** (11 Blaxland Rd; 9809 3496) and **North Sydney Bowling Club** (Ridge St; 9466 8896).

Part of the reason it may have caught on so well is that it must be the only sport that you can play and have a beer at the same time.

Rugby Reminiscing

What I used to love about rugby league games doesn't apply anymore because Norths have gone.

What I loved was sitting in the sun, drinking a beer, feeling the nervous buzz of chatter before your team ran out, hearing the great shock of noise as the players emerged pasted in so much liniment it made your eyes sting. Then the whistle and five minutes of frantic screaming, the cries of "Get 'em onside" and "They've been doing it all day" (screamed when a referee awards a decision in favour of your side – even if awarded in the first minute, you're bound to hear it). Then I liked the lull as you heard the barracking around you – some of it crude, some of it hilarious, some of it unintelligible. At the same time, when you were sitting on the hill you saw a constant stream of people moving around, some dressed in coats, some in thongs, some in ugg boots, all of them carrying beer or pies or soft drinks, or even those sugar-coated purple peanuts that you can't get anymore – a great mass of people often with nothing discernible to link them except a flash of colour and a cry of "Get 'em onside".

A lot of those elements are still there. The noise and the buzz when your side is doing well, the great leap in your chest that goes up to your throat, pulls you out of your chair and sets your mouth screaming when you see someone break the defensive line. The agony when your side knocks on, drops the ball, gives away a stupid penalty. The outrage at an incorrect decision, the general outrage at everything the refs do. Writing it down has made me want to go to a game this weekend. Would it be unfaithful of me to start supporting another team?

ANDREW HOBBS

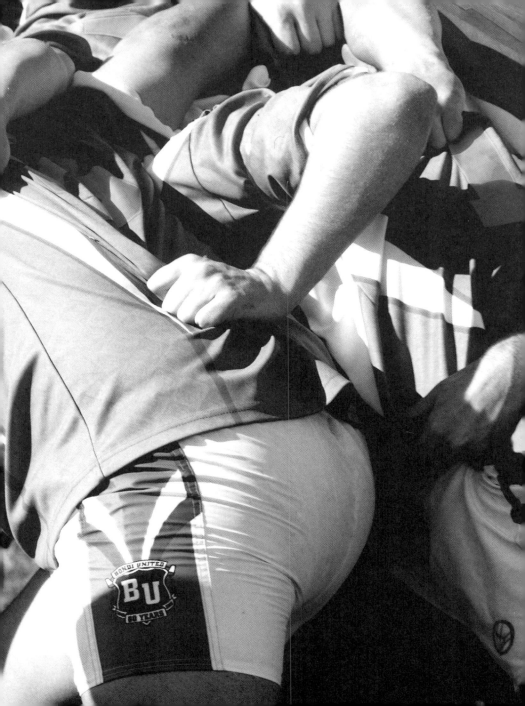

Slow Culture

There are a number of venues around town that are quintessentially Sydney – that over time have become part of the urban fabric. Some, like Baron's in Kings Cross, are disappearing, swallowed up by the property boom or changing demographics and interest, but thankfully other icons have managed to stick around.

As pubs opt for pokies rather than pop, live music is becoming increasingly hard to find in Sydney. Thank goodness for the **Basement** (*29 Reiby Place, Circular Quay*), which has been around since the early 70s and, even in the smoke-free noughties, retains its slightly louche atmosphere. It's dark and just a bit claustrophobic, slightly run-down, really is in a basement and manages to change its personality slightly every night depending on who's playing. People to have played here range from Nigel Kennedy to Billy Thorpe.

The **Griffin Theatre Company** (*10 Nimrod St, Kings Cross; www.griffintheatre.com.au*) was started in 1978 by NIDA graduates, including Robert Menzies and Penny Cook. It occupies a Kings Cross stables building, where it continues the tradition of its former occupants, the legendary Nimrod Theatre Company. Griffin dedicates itself to the development and production of new Australian plays. Cate Blanchett is said to have started her professional career here (although at least one other theatre, in Melbourne, makes the same claim), and films *Lantana*, *The Boys* and *The Heartbreak Kid* all began life as Griffin plays.

More than a century old, the **City Tattersalls Club** (*198-204 Pitt Street; www.city tatts.com.au*) is among the country's oldest racing clubs and happens to occupy one of the prime spots in the city. If you're too poor or principled to join an exclusive club, this is a pretty good option with six floors of restaurants, bars (some heritage listed), pools, gyms and various other rooms. Becoming a member is easy (just fill out a form and pay a nominal fee), and there's something deliciously decadent about being able to say: "Meet me at the club."

The photogenic **Hotel Hollywood** (*2 Foster St, Surry Hills*) has starred in numerous TV shows and has a former movie star as licensee. Doris Goddard worked with the likes of Katharine Hepburn and Peter Sellers before pulling beers in Surry Hills. The smell of greasepaint obviously isn't out of her blood; she's been known to entertain patrons with her own songs and poetry, and released an album, *Doris Goddard at Hotel Hollywood*.

It may have seen better days, but **Bondi Pavilion** (*Queen Elizabeth Drive, Bondi Beach*), built in 1928, is still to be celebrated. There's something about its colonnaded façade and upstairs deck looking to the horizon that reminds us that, once upon a time, being at the beach really was something exotic. It could do with a facelift, as long as its character isn't obliterated altogether. In the early days it housed Turkish baths, a ballroom and palm court, and was known as the 'Playground of the Pacific'; now you're more likely to find art exhibitions, plays, film festivals and pottery classes.

OK, so the seats aren't the most comfortable in the world, but with the demise of many inner-city theatres to make way for real estate over the past two or three decades, it's almost a miracle that the **Enmore Theatre** (*118-132 Enmore Rd, Newtown; www. enmoretheatre.com.au*) has survived. It was built in 1908 and extensively renovated in Art Deco style only 12 years later – Sydney's been make-over mad for almost a century, in case you didn't know. It's now classified by the National Trust as the only Art Deco theatre still in original condition (a euphemism for slightly run down, perhaps?) but that character-filled patina supplies just the right backdrop for stand-up comedy and Sydney's best bands.

Old Government House (*Parramatta Park; www.friendsofogh.com*) is Australia's oldest public building, constructed between 1799 and 1815, and was the rural residence of our early governors when they were trying to get away from the mean streets of filthy old Sydney. It's not quite so country anymore, but its position, on top of a hill overlooking the surrounding town and river, is quite spectacular.

The 100-hectare park used to be farmland for the house – there are remnants of the dairy and signs of where the vineyards used to be. The elegant Palladian-style mansion, is now looked after by the **National Trust** (*www.nswnationaltrust.org.au*) and part of it looks much as it would have done in Governor Macquarie's time. Visiting historic sites requires scones with jam and cream, we believe, and the restaurant in the courtyard behind the house doesn't disappoint. ∎

Eternity Man

Sydney's first and most prolific graffiti artist is a national treasure. The fact that Arthur Stace worked in chalk rather than spray paint probably added to his popularity, as did his determinedly one-tracked mind. For 35 years from 1932, Stace wrote the word 'Eternity' in beautiful copperplate on Sydney streets at least 50 times a day – all up, probably more than half a million times. Who did it and why was a mystery until Stace was identified in 1956. The WWI veteran, who'd grown up in poverty and been in jail at the age of 15, returned from the trenches half blind, an alcoholic and without a job. Life looked hopeless until he stumbled into East Sydney's Burton Street Baptist Tabernacle for a free meal, and heard a preacher shouting about eternity. The virtually illiterate Stace discovered his vocation. "I think 'Eternity' gets the message across," he told a reporter in 1965, two years before his death, "makes people stop and think." The chalk washed off decades ago, but Eternity found its way onto T-shirts, into lights on the Harbour Bridge for the millennium, into poems and even an opera. You could say, Eternity lives on.

GATHER
Shopping with Soul

--•--

"
WHAT VALUE DOES AN OBJECT HAVE WHEN YOU CAN
BUY 10 MORE EXACTLY THE SAME IN AN INSTANT?
"

Bernadette Murphy, *Zen and the Art of Knitting*

nurture

motion

travel

small

play

gather

Shopping and trade make the world go round, so we shouldn't feel guilty about embellishing our lives with whatever little luxuries we can afford. Maybe it's a handmade shirt, a bowl potted by a local artist, a pair of earrings rescued from a vintage era, a felted shawl or some other object into which time and love are poured that catches our attention and makes us open our wallet.

But allow ourselves to be corralled into sterile mall and sold mass-produced dross by surly, uninterested staff, and surely the beauty of shopping is lost. Blame convenience, or our propensity to be drawn towards global fads, but a myriad of small businesses and traditional stores have already been choked by the mass marketing mentality. The more we let it happen, the higher price we pay personally, culturally and collectively.

So shop with your heart. Buck the chain-store trend. Welcome stores that promote one-off clothing, art or homewares, or that recycle all of the above. Encourage the artist and the conscious consumer in yourself.

Shopping

Buy something you love from a tailor, an artist, a passionate collector or a corner shop, and you are stimulating local creativity, putting money back into your community and, along the way, interacting with others and having fun. More than the name on a credit card, you become the person who chooses local creations, gets to chat to knowledgeable and passionate staff, feels connected to the community and supports local businesses that, in turn, support you.

Fashion

If you want to turn back time, head to **Route 66** (225-257 Crown St, Darlinghurst; 9331 6686). Shopping in this 50s-focused store makes you feel like you've stepped onto the set of an old sitcom – you almost expect to see Fonzie in the corner slamming the jukebox. You can slip into a bowling shirt and go all out for a retro look, or pore over the recycled jewellery for a necklace or brooch that nanna forgot. Afterwards, there are plenty of places in Crown St to sit and watch the hip Darlo crowd go by.

Sooner or later every woman needs a hat. Former dancer and theatre milliner **Neil Grigg** (10 William St, Paddington; 9361 5864) has been a Sydney name for 20 years. Grigg can make a production-line hat for as little as $100, or something with vintage jewellery or semi-precious stones for up to $1500...or more. While you can buy some of his hats in

David Jones, see him in person for a perfectly tailored hat that will feel like it was designed for your shape and personality.

All the buttons – butterflies, bakelite, enamel, diamante and pearl-encrusted fasteners – at **Buttons, Buttons, Buttons** (25 Nurses Walk, the Rocks; 9252 0833) are so beautifully laid out that just peering at them through the glass is a pleasure in itself. This tiny shop sits in a historic arcade that was the precinct of Sydney's first hospital – used from 1788 to 1816. After it was abandoned, shops and dwellings took its place and by 1845, it became a bustling commercial area.

His unassuming manner and inherent shyness belie his international reputation as a formidable and unique talent. Sydneysider **Akira Isogawa** (12a Queen St, Woollahra; 9361 5221 and Level 2, the Strand Arcade; 9232 1078) designs one-off artisan pieces for women looking for floaty, feminine clothes,

Ties that Bind

Shane Rochefort of **Rochefort Ties** (*Shop C2, ground floor, 185 Elizabeth St; 9264 4408*) has around 2000 ties in his private collection. A tie, he says, "is a gentleman's personality – it's the last thing that gets put on and the first thing he'll be noticed for".

For the past five years, Rochefort, who used to work in publishing, has been making ties out of fabrics of his own designs. Inspiration, he says, can come from anywhere – a swatch of his grandmother's wallpaper, an examination of 130 years of paisley patterns and books on architectural history.

He works out of a shop, very discreetly tucked away inside an office building, full of antiques and lovely artwork, books with names like *Canes Through the Ages* and sample boards of designs. A busy day, he says, is if he has half a dozen customers – personal service is paramount.

Apart from being thoroughly obsessed with these particular lengths of fabric, the tie business came about because he wasn't entirely satisfied with any of his vintage ones. "Each tie has its good and bad points – it might have been a great design but in light material, or in the best fabric but too spare. I'd think if only it could be a little bit like this or more like that, imagine how good it could be."

After much research, Rochefort worked out that jacquard weave, with its depth, texture and weight, was an essential element. The best silk jacquard, he discovered, comes from Como, in Italy; there, he found three loomers who could translate his designs, including one who resurrected a loom that had lain unused for 70 years. More recently, he has also been using an English company for his twills and club colours.

A Rochefort tie, with the brand embroidered along its edge, wrapped in specially printed tissue paper and packaged in an exquisite box, is a work of art, so much so that each is numbered, just like a limited edition print. Rochefort now also does bespoke shirt-making and tailoring (the suits are lined in the same gorgeous silks as the ties) and has a special service in which he makes ties to fit – extra long for "the taller gent, slightly wider for someone else – I cut a pattern to fit, and then have it on file for the next time he comes in".

as well as costumes for the Sydney Dance Company and players in the Australian Chamber Orchestra.

Isogawa's philosophy is that "a garment can transcend; giving it a soul. I translate fabrics into soft and romantic silhouettes, using natural fabrics like silks and cottons, which are kind to the skin". He works with textile specialists who hand appliqué and bead fabric for his exquisite creations. He handpaints, embroiders and handstitches garments, imbuing each with an individual touch. If you have the cash, a piece by Akira is guaranteed to be not only wearable but also collectable.

The whole concept of the **Graduate Store** *(Shop 103, Level 2 the Strand, 412-414 George St; 9233 4413)* is appealing. Six recent graduates of TAFE's Fashion Design Studio have been handpicked by head teacher Nicholas Huxley and set up in the shop. It's stocked with the designers' ready-to-wear labels; each works there one day a week, and they all work together on the nitty-gritty of running a business. After a year or so six new graduates are brought in, to give another bunch of fledgling designers a start. The clothes are fresh, sophisticated and very wearable…and there's a chance that you may be picking up an early work of a big name of the future.

Vintage clothing fans looking for one-off pieces should head where stylists shop for photo shoots, **Grandma Takes a Trip** *(263 Crown St, Surry Hills; 9356 3322 or 79 Gould St, Bondi Beach; 9130 6262; www.grand matakesatrip.com.au)* specialises in clothes from the 50s, 60s and 70s and everything is arranged in helpful colour stories so you don't have to search too long for something that suits. The shop recently launched a new range, Handcrafted by Grandma, a collection of dresses, slips, boleros and summer coats made from vintage fabric.

A must-see for vintage jewellery lovers is **Margo Richards Antiques** *(27 Nurses Walk, the Rocks; 9252 2855)*. Yes, it's a more than a little pricey – *Italian Vogue* editor Anna Piaggi is reported to shop here when in Sydney – but the Venetian foil beads, diamante brooches, beaded purses, glittering shawls and even bejewelled hair pins are well worth the price tag. They'll make you feel like the glitteratti, even if you don't work for a glossy magazine.

Homewares

There are rug showrooms and rug showrooms, and then there's **TibetSydney** *(22 Queen St, Woollahra; 9363 2588)*, which is run by Diki Ongmo, a Tibetan with a degree in comparative religions who has lived everywhere from New York to Darjeeling. She runs the business with her partner, architectural photographer Tim Linkins.

The first thing you'll most likely notice about the shop, which is set in a Woollahra terrace, is its highly unusual timber portal and very un-Sydney like contemporary but calming interior, designed by the internationally recognised Brisbane-based architects, Donovan Hill. It would be worth visiting TibetSydney just to marvel over the jewel box of a space, with its bamboo garden and oriental pond, but you'll soon discover the attention to detail runs right through to the rugs as well – gorgeous pieces, handcrafted in Kathmandu, which often feature surprising twists on traditional designs.

Eclectic/ Specialists

Spend some time in quirky little shops that remind you it's about the experience, not just the end result.

Mrs Red & Sons (*427 Crown St Surry Hills; 9310 4860*) is a corner shop where the delicate finds in its window are displayed like rare jewels. There's not a lot but everything in their diminutive Asian-inspired range – from chopsticks to noodle bowls, incense and tiny ornaments – is adorable. Best of all, everything you buy, down to the most humble purchase, is wrapped almost origami style by the charming owners, with your change delivered on a silver tray.

You don't have to be a Steiner devotee to enjoy the minuscule **Rudolf Steiner Book Centre** (*307 Sussex St; 9264 5169*) on the edge of Chinatown. It's full of beautiful handmade toys, interesting children's books and outstanding art materials, including waxes, pencils and paints. And it's the only place we know of that sells beeswax birthday candles.

Parkers Art Supplies (*3 Cambridge St, the Rocks; 9247 9979*) is an artwork in itself, with jars of perfectly pointed brushes, mesmerising displays of tubed paints, luscious sticks of pastel and shelves and shelves of art papers. It's been around since 1918 and even if your artistic ability peaked in primary school, there's something about this place that makes you thrill even at the sight of a paintbox.

The friendly **Da Capo Music** (*upstairs at 51 Glebe Point Rd, Glebe; 9660 1825*) is the place for second-hand sheet music and books about music, including biographies of composers and concert programmes. There are also unusual finds; everything from a violin duet, self-published by a US professor and dedicated to his wife, to a funny old book of ukulele tunes.

Handmade

Perhaps it's a response to fast, mass production, or maybe we're just craving goods with a bit of character, but there's a growing movement in Sydney towards handmade and lovingly crafted.

The **Society of Arts & Crafts of NSW** (*104 George St, the Rocks; 9241 5825*) was established in 1906 by six artists who wanted to promote local quality handcrafts that were inspired by the colours and motifs they found around them.

Today the society shows off its work to locals and tourists from a historic building in the Rocks, which is the earliest surviving Coroners Court in NSW. It makes a delightful backdrop to the huge variety of work crafted by artists from all over Sydney, working with all sorts of materials from fabric to gold.

There are some one hundred members of the society and they each take turns tending the shop, so you can get a first-hand explanation of the work that you are buying. Keep an eye out for Columbian-born Martha Catano's joyful embroidered textile collages in naive artform that show scenes from Australian life. All her work is completed on an old Singer sewing machine. Potter Jan O'Connell does blackfired bowls and platters; Helen Thomas is a textile artist who knits, spins and weaves alpaca and wool clothing; and Ksenija Benko creates Art Nouveau–style enamel, opal, pearl and silver jewellery.

At **Kraft Handmade Homewares** (*431 King St, Newtown; 9557 9845*) owner Nita Moore has an eye for fun and for treasures, and you can buy handmade diaries embroidered with fabric, silk scarfs, handmade dolls and even photo albums made from mulberry trees.

My, my, my, my, my Boogie Shoes

I can't dance. I have no sense of rhythm, and as a kid I was too chubby for ballet.
I felt like a fraud going into Salvio's Dancing Shoes at Randwick. But when I went to a fiesta at Diana Reyes Flamenco Studio in Newtown, I was desperate to know where all the dancers had bought their shoes. Everyone else was signing up for lessons, but I knew that was a lost cause.

Salvio's Dancing Shoes *(34 St Paul's St, Randwick; 9398 3502)* is one of the last places in Australia that makes dancing shoes and, perhaps surprisingly, you'll find it tucked away in a little group of shops near the Randwick Ritz, not in any specialist arcade.

There's nothing slick about Salvio's. It has been going since 1881 in the same family and, as far as anyone can tell, is the oldest dance shoe company in the world. It's one of those old-fashioned, slightly matter-of-fact shoe shops with serious-looking foot measures and wallpaper that went up 25 years ago. Samples of all their shoes are on display – tap shoes, ballet shoes, flamenco shoes and every other type of dancing shoes there might be.

Upstairs is the workshop, where they handmake about 20,000 pairs of shoes a year; from where you can hear faint hammering and the odd big clunk. Clients have included Opera Australia and the Moscow Circus.

The ballet pumps are sweet – lovely, birthday-candle pink satin with a sliver of leather on the sole – and tempting. I'll just have the flamenco shoes. "What colour do you want them?" she asks me. I could have gone through their supply of leather if I'd wanted something special. I start thinking about burgundy suede. But I go for Salvio's standard black. "Do you want nails?" Yes, I'd love to walk down the street clicking and clacking. "Oh, you're not going to wear them for dancing? You'd better not have nails, or the neighbours will hate you." Ten days later I get a call to say my shoes are ready. Perfect, handmade fat-heeled shoes, lined with leather and with 'Made in Australia' on the leather soles. I've never had a blister from them and am often stopped on the street by people wanting to know my source. But I still can't dance.

LETA KEENS

HORUS

io's

G SHOES

CHORUS

io's

SHOES

'S STRAP

CAMEL 390 CHORUS

Salvio's

6 DANCING SHOES

Buying secondhand, 'green', or sustainable products is a wonderful way to care about the city and community in which you live. There's less waste and more love.

The brainchild of 30-year-old Sydney entrepreneur Danin Kahn, **Todae** *(83 Glebe Point Rd, Glebe; 1300 138 483)* purveys just about everything you might need for a more sustainable lifestyle. Shelves are stocked with organic cotton bedding, recycled paper, boots made from tyres and textiles from the streets of Brazil, toxin-free paint and even biodegradable, reusable plates made of bamboo fibre.

There's a huge range of power-saving lightbulbs, and it turns out that simple water-saving devices like shower timers are best-sellers with "conscientious city dwellers" and "retirees who want to give back". Danin's own lifestyle is carbon neutral, and he and his staff can offer all the advice and practical help you'll need to be your own shade of greenie.

With a name like **Planet** *(419 Crown St, Surry Hills; 9698 0680)*, it's no surprise that Ross Longmuir's philosophy for his shop "is to make the world a better place". Part of the Surry Hills scene since 1998, Planet is lends a little glamour to this section. It's a refreshing antidote to mass production, and an oddly contrasting sense of calm and exhilaration pervades this two-storey terrace. For a start there's the wonderfully simple and sophisticated Australian hardwood furniture Longmuir himself designs. In the ever-changing room settings throughout are works by many of the 70 or so makers from Australia and overseas, all of whom make beautifully crafted objects out of real and sustainable materials.

Longmuir, who studied psychology before turning to furniture making, has a simple philosophy when it comes to retailing: "If I wouldn't have it in my own home, I wouldn't stock it, even if I knew it would sell." A second branch of Planet, at 114 Commonwealth St, Surry Hills, acts more like a gallery and features collectibles as well as other furniture by Longmuir.

Another stylish place where you needn't feel guilty about splurging is **Grok** *(97 Military Rd, Neutral Bay; 9908 5411)*. Bowls, baskets, toys, bags, jewellery, candles and anything else you can imagine are sourced from Fair Trade and other community organisations, and often made from environmentally friendly or recycled materials. There's a very sweet little cafe in the bamboo courtyard, too – doing good works never felt so good.

Everything in **m.a.d.** *(55 Enmore Rd, Newtown; 9557 3411)* – which stands for Make a Difference – is made from recycled objects and mostly by young designers. It has fantastic jewellery and fashion accessories, including belts made from bike tyres. More accurately it might be described as a Sustainable Art & Design Centre.

It was created by the not-for-profit cooperative **Reverse Garbage** *(142 Addison Rd, Marrickville; 9569 3132)*, which has been giving junk a good name for more than three decades. They sell industrial discards, offcuts and over-runs, and you never know what you might find here – anything from a store mannequin or an office chair to hessian sacks or jewellery bits and pieces. Artists and designers love the place, and the cooperative recently started the fabulous 'Junk Love' re-use art and design competition, which inspired people to think creatively about their consumption and excess.

If you're looking for the weird, the wonderful, the stylish, the kitsch and, of course, the pre-loved, get yourself to **Newtown Old Wares** (*439 King St, Newtown; 9519 6705*), a cornucopia of vintage homewares specialising in "Deco to Disco, 40s to 70s". That means an old beach bucket with Disney characters decorating the outside, a Flip Clock radio and Black Lady Lamps.

Across the road at **Vintage Delight** (*488 King St, Newtown; 9550 2407*), owner Grace Kassim is a little fussier about what comes and goes, perhaps because the shop is more compact and the clientele more specialised. This is the place where photography aficionados will stumble upon a 1937 Kodak Jiffy, for example, or those fascinated with naval knick-knacks will find a Morse Key dating from 1900. Our personal favourites: a Mickey Mouse Club Annual, the Kewpie dolls, English top hats and Skippy ashtrays.

In the enormous emporium, **Mona Vale Salvation Army** (*1 Bungan Court; 9999 5735*), you'll find inexpensive china, lovely old embroidered tablecloths, records and toys, not to mention furniture that won't break the bank.

While you're on the northern beaches, it's worth dropping into the **Newport Red Cross Shop** (*334 Barrenjoey Rd; 9979 1738*). It's very small and you'll have to poke around, but you may just find a real treasure. The volunteers running this op shop are particularly nice.

You should also visit the **Antique General Store** (*2 Warraba Rd, Narrabeen; 9913 7636*), which is set in an old house, with each room displaying the works of a different dealer and ranging from oak desks and chandeliers to pocket handkerchiefs. It has a really good turnover, which means there'll be a different feel each time you visit.

Finish up with a trip to **Avalon Red Cross Shop** (*48 Old Barrenjoey Rd; 9918 0952*). We've uncovered loads of top-quality goods here, including some fabulous Scandinavian glasses.

No mention of Sydney's secondhand shops would be complete without the eastern suburbs' first port of call for recycling, **Paddington Salvation Army** (*292 Oxford St*). Pre-loved furniture and home accessories, as well as clothes and shoes from labels such as Diesel, Karen Walker and Calibre, compete for space in this store frequented by upmarket and downtrodden bargain hunters.

Trash or Treasure

Check local council websites to find out household clean-up collection dates – a brilliant (and free) way to pick up some gems in the way of furniture, plants and who knows what else. You'll be reducing your eco footprint and gathering special finds. And the Australian Conservation Foundation (*www.acfonline.org.au*) is a font of information on the best places to dispose of your excess.

Hear Australian writer Tim Winton talk about his masterful *Cloud Street* or American Robert Crais give the lowdown on his tough guy with a heart of gold hero Elvis Cole at the colourful Sydney institution **Gleebooks** *(49 Glebe Point Rd, Glebe; 9660 2333)*. Set in a two-storey terrace, this bookshop is the design antithesis of the chain stores and stands out as one of the city's best. The aisles are packed with books on politics, arts, design and environmental issues, as well as fiction titles. You can linger here, find books you thought were long lost, or make conversation with the other clientele – a mixture of university students, alternative lifestylers and intellectuals.

One of those lovely old-fashioned bookshops that's more into content than slick display, **Abbey's Bookshop** *(131 York St; 9264 3111)* is the kind of place where you know you'll find exactly what you're looking for, whether that's the latest fiction or a philosophy text. It's close to Town Hall station, so it's perfect if you need a book to read on the train home. And if you're looking for something in Swahili, the Language Book Centre upstairs is just the ticket.

Kinokuniya *(Level 2, the Galeries Victoria, 500 George St; 9262 7996)* is huge and has the best selection of design and art books you're likely to find. This Japanese bookshop also has one of the broadest collections of fiction around, particularly by American authors. Great for stationery and pens too…and, of course, plenty of Japanese books.

Set in a modern extension to the exceedingly beautiful Italianate Tusculum Villa (built in the 1830s and now headquarters of the NSW chapter of the Royal Australian Institute of Architects), **Architext** *(3 Manning St, Potts Point; 9356 2022)* is the place for books on architecture and landscape design, or just to experience some outstanding Sydney architecture.

Make a Day of It

Too often shopping feels like just another chore. But why not do it the old-fashioned way, get dressed up for your retail adventure and take it slowly? Plan on a delicious, mid-shopping lunch or a decadent afternoon tea. Take along a friend for conversation, a second opinion or to share in the experience. Discover new treasures through each other's eyes.

You don't have to have a million dollars to enjoy your spree. Linger over a beautifully crafted item, or even things your budget won't stretch to but in which you can still see the skill and art. Talk to the people selling the goods about where they came from or how they were made. Savour the idea that something that might have sat in an artists' studio, or even someone else's home if you're buying recycled, will soon be loved by you. Only ever buy things you love.

Markets

There are a few surprises among the tourist fodder at the compact **Manly Markets** *(lower end of Sydney Rd adjacent to the Corso; 9am-5pm Sat and Sun)*, like the elegant pictures made of paper cuttings, the handmade dog coats for pampered canines and the vibrant, hand-dyed silk scarfs and sarongs. Perhaps you'll fancy a black-and-white or colour photograph from French snapper Thomas Joannes, or some pungently scented carrot and mandarin or coconut soap from natural cosmetics maker Fluff & Bubbles. No matter how many times you visit, you'll always find something new to delight, often inspired by the local landscape, culture or lifestyle.

You'll find arts and crafts, clothing, jewellery, plants and much more at **Balmain Markets** *(cnr Darling St and Curtis Rd; 8.30am-4pm Sat)*, which has a trendy yet laid-back vibe that is distinct to this inner-city suburb. Although squeezed into the grounds of an old local church, the market boasts a beautiful tree-filled courtyard in which to rest mid-forage.

If it's going to be in fashion, it will arrive at **Bondi Beach Markets** *(Bondi Beach Public School, cnr Campbell Pde and Warners Ave; 9am-4pm Sun)*. Designers Sass + Bide got their start at a beachside stall, and visiting celebrities often swing past to see what's cooking on the local scene. It stocks everything from clothing to old records. Later, head along the main street to the New Zealand ice-cream shop and lick a hokey-pokey cone in the sun.

Get a massage, a vegetarian snack, or some very funky second-hand clothes at the chilled-out and colourful **Glebe Market** *(Glebe Public School, cnr Glebe Point Rd and Derby Place; 9am-4pm Sat)*. And if that's not quite relaxed enough for your Saturday morning, you can retire to the adjoining park for some bongoes and basking.

Easily Sydney's busiest market, **Paddington Bazaar** *(Oxford St; 10am-4pm Sat)* has everything from clothing and jewellery to artwork, homewares, aromatherapy oils, plants and more. Don't let the push and shove distract you from wallowing in the wares. When it's time for a breather, sit and listen to one of the many buskers.

A genuine flea market, **Rozelle Markets** *(Rozelle Public School, Darling St; 9am-4pm Sat and Sun)* has been running for 15 years. The beauty of Rozelle is that the vibe's good all day, not just early in the morning. If you want to compete with the dealers, get there before 8am.

Shopping is usually the last thing on your mind when you visit a museum (although many of the gallery and museum shops are fantastically eclectic). But a couple of times of year, usually around August and before Christmas, **Young Blood Designers Market** *(www.powerhousemuseum.com)* is reason enough to visit the Powerhouse Museum when around 40 mostly new and local designers show off their wares, in everything from furniture to fashion.

The 'curated market' (translates as 'no rubbish'), in the basement of the building, is a great place to find out what's happening in a whole range of design fields, including fashion, bags and jewellery, furniture and lighting, and pick up some amazing bargains along the way (one Young Blood happens conveniently close to Christmas to solve all your present-buying dilemmas). ∎

Arcades

Perhaps what makes the Strand Arcade (pictured) such a favourite is that, although located off the busy hub of Pitt St, outside lunchtime it remains a tranquil oasis. It's also the place to imagine you are in times of old, as well as find something special. A rare, rebuilt late Victorian arcade from the prosperous 'boom' times between 1880 and 1900, the Strand was inspired by London's successful Burlington Arcade. You can almost imagine the gentry swinging their canes and swirling their umbrellas as they shopped. The merchandise of today ranges from designer clothes and lingerie to chocolate shops and chemical-free skincare.

You'll find much of the same in the Queen Victoria Building *(George St)* but it doesn't really matter what you come for; it's the elegant Romanesque architecture by stonemasons, plasterers and stained-window artists, and the animated Royal Clock featuring the Battle of Hastings and hourly execution of King Charles I that will keep drawing you back. Designed by George McRae and completed in 1898, the QVB replaced the original Sydney markets on the site. It fills an entire city block bound by George, Market, York and Druitt Sts. Even if you don't buy something, it is the perfect place for whiling away a wet afternoon.

Index

Features & boxed texts

Slow-mos